Color & Texture

Color & Texture

Decorative Expressions for Today's Home

Jessica Elin Hirschman, Ellen M. Plante,
Ann Rooney Heuer, Penelope O'Sullivan

MetroBooks

MetroBooks

An Imprint of Friedman/Fairfax Publishers

Library of Congress Cataloging-in-Publication Data available upon request.

ISBN 1-58663-031-8

Editors: Hallie Einhorn, Dana Rosen, and Reka Simonsen
Art Director: Jeff Batzli
Designers: Charles Donahue, Meredith Miller, Jennifer O'Connor, and Lynne Yeamans
Photography Editors: Erin Feller, Valerie Kennedy, and Christopher C. Bain
Production Managers: Camille Lee, Leslie Wong, and Karen Matsu Greenberg

Color separations by Fine Arts Repro House Co., Ltd.
Printed in China by Leefung-Asco Printing Limited

1 3 5 7 9 10 8 6 4 2

For bulk purchases and special sales, please contact:
Friedman/Fairfax Publishers
Attention: Sales Department
15 West 26th Street
New York, NY 10010
212/685-6610   FAX 212/685-1307

Visit our website:
www.metrobooks.com

Contents

Introduction

In home design—as in other visual arts—form, color, and texture are key elements of expression. While form shapes the structure of our surroundings, color and texture affect the mood. These latter elements can also alter our perceptions regarding form, making big spaces seem cozy, and tight ones appear airy and light. By exploring the chapters in this book, you can learn how to manipulate color and texture to create attractive, harmonious environments throughout your home.

In a well-designed room, color and texture work as a team, each helping to bring the other to life. Together, they have the power to transform ordinary spaces into remarkable settings. Picture a bedroom with wallpaper bearing a rosy floral print, a brass bed topped by a delicate white crocheted coverlet, and windows adorned with gauzy white curtains. The overall effect is one of pure romance. However, replace the sheer window treatment with heavy velvety drapes and the feel of the room is completely altered.

Color itself has the power to thrill. Indoors, vivid hues create exciting backdrops for furniture, while outdoors, they provide powerful accents in both shady and sunny settings. One of the most obvious ways of introducing color into a room is through paint, which opens up a world of possibilities. Not only are there limitless hues to choose from, but there are differences in sheen and numerous painting techniques as well. A faux marble paint treatment may be just the thing you need to give your front entrance that sense of refinement. Or a textured paint treatment may be the perfect complement to the traditional decor of your living room. And paint is not just for walls. Jazz up those old wooden floorboards with a checkerboard pattern, or create the illusion of a rug with a clever painted design.

Of course, paint is not the only means for adding color to a room. There are all sorts of decorative aspects to consider, from upholstery and window treatments to flooring and rugs. And don't forget the furnishings themselves.

Opposite: BATHERS ARE SURE TO FIND REST AND RELAXATION IN THIS SETTING, THANKS TO A SOOTHING PALETTE OF BLUE AND WHITE REMINISCENT OF A PEACEFUL SKY. WHILE PAINTED WHITE SHUTTERS PROVIDE PRIVACY AT THE WINDOWS, GAUZY WHITE VALANCES MAINTAIN THE AIRY FEEL OF THE SPACE. FRESH FLOWERS SCATTERED THROUGHOUT INTRODUCE NATURAL TEXTURE AND MAKE THE ROOM EVEN MORE INVITING.

Above: A STRIKING PURPLE PAINT TREATMENT ENSURES THAT THE HEARTH IS THE FOCAL POINT OF THIS LIVING ROOM. SUBTLE VARIATIONS IN TONE RESULT IN A SOFTENING EFFECT, PREVENTING THE WALL FROM SEEMING OVERPOWERING. **Opposite:** A RUGGED STONE WALL CREATES A FLATTERING BACKDROP FOR AN ARRAY OF COLLECTIBLES IN EARTHY HUES. THE UNEVEN SURFACE PROVIDES WELCOME CONTRAST TO THE SMOOTH CERAMIC TILES OF THE COUNTERTOP.

When deciding on a color scheme, many decorators turn to nature for inspiration. Nature's spectrum of colors and textures is broad, with hues ranging from the ocher and sienna of the earth to the blue of the sky and the green of the trees. Foliage itself comes in many shades—blue-green, blackish, gold, lime-green, gray-green, deep forest green, red, and even purple. Add to leaf shades the colorful variety of quarried stone and marble available for home use and the options for a nature-based palette become infinite.

Neutrals, such as taupe, beige, cream, gray, and white, are also part of nature's palette. And they aren't as bland as the word "neutral" might imply. Elegant and urbane, neutrals imbue the rooms they grace with a feeling of serenity. Texture becomes especially important in spaces decorated with these hues, as it provides variety without being disruptive. Imagine the reflective gleam of a polished taupe travertine tabletop, the tight bumpy weave of a nubby beige rug, and the cool, clean crispness of white cotton sheets. The different textures add substance and weight to these varied forms.

Harvest hues, like neutrals, have an enduring place in home design. Stained wood, an accent in many color schemes, comes into its own in this color range. Paneling, ceiling beams, flooring, and furnishings are a few of the forms in which wood manifests itself and assumes importance. In addition to wood, Oriental rugs made from natural dyes; comfortable seats upholstered in brown or burgundy leather; and a brick, granite, or carved limestone hearth can contribute to a cozy, earthy room.

Blue and white is a classic color combination that has long experienced tremendous popularity and continues to strike a chord with many. This charming duo exudes a freshness and uplifting quality unlike any other palette. Highly versatile, the combination can be either sophisticated or demure—it's the tone or shade that makes the difference. Cerulean blue paired with soft white recalls a tranquil sky with puffy clouds. A combination of brilliant turquoise and bright white, on the other hand, suggests a tropical seascape. On the exterior of a home, a blue front door with white trim or blue shutters against a white facade will provide an immediate link to nature and the

Right: AN ENCHANTING NATURE-INSPIRED PALETTE OF SOFT GREEN AND CREAMY WHITE INFUSES THIS SUNROOM WITH A GARDENLIKE AIR. THE NATURAL LOOK IS ENHANCED BY THE INCORPORATION OF WOOD FURNISHINGS AND POTTED PLANTS. NOTICE HOW THE FLOWERS IN THE VASE ECHO THE COLOR SCHEME OF THE SETTING.

sky above. This color pairing can also appear outdoors in patio furniture, tile fountains, and garden flowers.

Contrasting textures and colors defeat monotony. To play up fine architectural moldings, paint them a different color from the main wall surface. A cream-colored cornice, for example, provides pleasant contrast to dark green walls and helps open up the space. Plus, the extra dimension of the molding adds interest. In a monochromatic room, create visual distinctions by varying textures. Velvet slipcovers, brightly polished marble, plush carpets, and a wool tapestry with various smooth, tufted, and knotted areas will bring rich contrast to such a space.

Texture not only injects variety but also affects our perception of color. A rough stucco wall appears darker than a smooth wall because the little depressions and raised surfaces of the former create shadows. Smooth surfaces, such as polished granite and walls with enamel paints, reflect light and, in turn, make colors appear lighter. Thus, using too many shiny objects in a room can create a hard, comfortless environment, while a dark room with heavily textured objects can seem leaden and dull.

When used with sensitivity, stone and marble add earthiness and warmth to a room. These materials work well for floors, counters, and walls in both kitchens and baths. A foyer can also benefit from stone flooring, which stands up to heavy traffic and dirt. In a living room, a stone fireplace can provide a dramatic focal point. A hearth composed of rough-hewn stone will contribute an informal tone, while a carved stone mantel will add gravity and formality.

Outdoors, locally quarried materials usually look best. For instance, in northern New England, the granite rocks of the landscape are often the building blocks of choice, while in the Cotswold area of England, dwellings are constructed of the golden limestone local to that region. In general, weathered stone has a stronger appeal than newly quarried stone. And lichens and moss add a timeless quality to rocks while making structures seem all the more at home in their natural surroundings.

Not only does outdoor stonework look better with a regional slant, but exterior paint colors also benefit from taking the location into consideration. The quality of sunlight has a powerful effect on the appearance of paint colors. In southern California, for example, intense golden sunlight enhances such colors as saturated red, yellow, purple, orange, and electric blue, while low-key colors fade to insignificance. The brighter colors find their way onto gates, doors, moldings, garden furniture, and garden ornaments. In New Hampshire's more subdued northerly atmosphere, light gray, muted yellow, grayish blue, and dark forest green suit the less intense light and appear with regularity on clapboards, doors, gates, and shutters.

Although the outside of a house may sometimes clue you into the decor of the interior, this is not always the case. Adventurous homeowners often break decorating rules with great success. Use this book to help you experiment, have fun, and try new combinations of color and texture to achieve the look you want.

—*Penelope O'Sullivan*

PART ONE

PAINT & COLOR

INTRODUCTION

Great color schemes have been inspired by a wide variety of sources both likely and unlikely, from the bold contrasts of a modernist painting to the plays of light typical of a cloudy day. Nature abounds with subtle and vivid palettes, with landscapes providing visual lessons in how different colors can be combined without overpowering individual hues. History is equally rich in stimuli. Books depicting ancient civilizations, art and design movements of the past, or contemporary foreign cultures can all offer inspiration. Museums, home furnishing magazines, and even jewelry are also rich sources of ideas for new color combinations.

The range of color available today is remarkable. The colors used in the interior and exterior spaces of a home should, most importantly, reflect the tastes and preferences of the inhabitants. However, there are a few basic guidelines that govern the use of color in home design. Easily understood and mastered, these principles open

up the enormous potential of the world of color.

COLOR THEORY BASICS

Color theory is best understood through reference to the color wheel, which was devised by the seventeenth-century physicist Sir Isaac Newton as a graphic representation of how colors relate to one another visually and scientifically. The ordering of colors on the color wheel corresponds to the rainbow. Complementary colors lie directly opposite one another on the wheel; analogous colors are adjacent.

The three terms that describe color are hue, value, and saturation. Hue refers to the position a color occupies

Left: TEXTURED SURFACES ABSORB AND REFLECT LIGHT DIFFERENTLY FROM FLAT SURFACES, SUBTLY CHANGING THE PERCEPTIONS AND FEEL OF APPLIED COLOR. FOUND CHAIRS, CAREFULLY SANDED AND PAINTED TO HIDE WEAR AND TEAR, APPEAR CREAMY. THE COLORS SEEM SOFT. BY CONTRAST, THE PAINTED FENCE DERIVES ITS VISUAL INTEREST FROM THE ROUGH-HEWN SURFACE THAT SUITS ITS NATURAL AND EARTHY HUES. **Above:** DIFFERENT SHADES OF PINK REVEAL HOW COLOR CAN ENHANCE TEXTURE. A LIGHT SHADE OF PINK ON THE TOP HALF OF THIS GARDEN WALL OUTLINES THE SHAPE AND TEXTURE OF THE BRICKS. A SLIGHTLY DARKER SHADE MAKES THE BOTTOM APPEAR SMOOTHER BY CONTRAST.

on the color wheel and is synonymous with its name, such as red, yellow, or blue. Value describes the lightness or darkness of a color and is used interchangeably with tone. Colors of equal value or tone appear as the identical gray in black-and-white photographs. Saturation is the intensity or brightness of a color, with highly saturated colors usually appearing richer and fuller.

In color lexicons, hues are discussed as warm or cool. This phraseology relates to the fact that light radiates heat—the more light, the more heat. Red hues are considered the hottest colors. Conversely, blues are described as the coolest colors. Green, made by mixing blue and yellow, can be considered a warm or cool color, depending upon how it is used. The degree of warmth or coolness of any color is relative; there are cooler shades of red and warmer blues. It all depends upon the proportion of the hues mixed to achieve that particular shade and what other hues surround that shade.

CHOOSING AND COMBINING COLOR

The human eye can discern as many as ten million colors. Selecting even a few hues for a color scheme can be confusing, and this task is complicated by the fact that the perception of a color changes depending upon many fac-

tors: the amount and quality of light, the texture of a painted surface, the finish of a paint selected, and even the eye of the observer. The best way to know how a color will look in a particular room is to tape samples to a wall and leave them there for a few days, checking to see how the color looks at different times of the day. There are also a few guidelines to keep in mind.

*Lighter colors create a sense of openness and make a room seem larger, whereas darker colors bring the walls closer and make a room seem smaller and cozier. Bright colors can be cheery and uplifting, while deeper tones can have a somber effect upon a room, although today's popular jewel tones often evoke an Old World ambiance rich in spirit.

*Bright colors will generally appear more vivid in strong light. Warm colors can compensate for a lack of light and therefore can be used to cheer up north-facing or cooler rooms, while cool colors can make a warm room feel more temperate and comfortable. Rooms with constantly changing light, such as east- and west-facing spaces, are vulnerable to glare and intermittently intense exposures of light. A good choice for these rooms is a neutral blended from a combination of whites and strong hues; as the light changes, this color will pick up different

undertones that will change how the color is perceived. A wall that looks yellowish in the morning may appear whiter at midday and violet or translucent at twilight.

*Cool colors often appear to be receding and thus give a sense of depth to a space. Warm colors, on the other hand, visually bring surfaces closer because they appear to advance. Balancing an equal number of warm and cool colors is a very effective way to make a multihued palette appear as one cohesive scheme rather than a mixture of competing elements.

*Interior color schemes are referred to as related or contrasting. The former includes monochromatic schemes, which consist of varying tones and intensities of one hue, and analogous schemes, which consist of colors adjacent to one another on the color wheel. Complements and other contrasting color schemes can provide very dramatic effects, but they can still look harmonious when the hues are of the same saturation or value.

*A good way to add a feeling of cohesiveness to a room or a series of rooms is to paint the walls, ceiling, and trim the same hue. For example, painting interior trim throughout a house the same color optically minimizes the distance and separation between spaces. Conversely, selecting a different color for each room will visually separate the spaces.

A lavish use of color can open up a whole world of new decorating opportunities. The following pages present a wealth of fresh, invigorating ideas for using color inside and outside the home.

Above: COLOR AND CREATIVITY COMBINE IN THIS OCEANSIDE HOUSE. IN KEEPING WITH THE HOME'S LAID-BACK SURFER THEME, ARCHITECT BRIAN MURPHY USED ORDINARY STRAW DOORMATS—PAINTED IN WARM TROPICAL COLORS—TO CREATE AN UNUSUAL AND CASUAL SIDE TABLE.

Palettes, Moods, and Architecture

As a design tool, color is immensely powerful because of its ability to change the look and feel of a room. Color can alter a room's architecture in many ways: by enhancing beautiful detail, compensating for a lack of architectural character or masking undesirable features, imposing scale, or delineating space. And the palette — the overall color scheme — chosen for a room is perhaps the single most important element in establishing its mood.

Color can be its own geometry, reshaping the boundaries of conventional construction by changing the manner in which the proportions of room are perceived. Consider the primary colors as an example. Because reds and other warm colors appear to be advancing, they can make walls seem closer and a large room appear more demure. Yellow is perceived as the natural color of light and generally makes a room feel more spacious. Blues, which fall at the cool end of the color spectrum, often look as though they are receding, making walls look farther away and a room appear larger. Color can also emphasize particular architectural elements within a room, such as an unusually shaped wall or handsome trim, or create a new geometry composed of the juxtaposition of hues.

Every hue imparts its own personality to the room in which it is used. The palettes featured on the following pages reveal how paint and color can impact tangibly and intangibly on the character of many different spaces.

Left: It is believed that blue, particularly dark shades, enhances the ability to remember dreams. Bright accent colors and a white duvet cover keep this predominantly blue palette from overwhelming the small bedroom. **Above left:** Yellow is perceived as the natural color of light. Here, yellow walls reflect the morning sunlight streaming through the windows and brighten the room. **Above right:** Red rooms get noticed. In this dining room, artificial illumination supplied by candles emphasizes the warmth of the deep red walls, making it the perfect setting for entertaining and engaging in lively conversation.

Right: THE FOCAL POINT OF THIS FAMILY ROOM IS THE CUSTOM-DESIGNED DOUBLE-SIDED FIREPLACE. ARCHITECT JEFFREY TOHL CALLS ATTENTION TO THE UNUSUAL SCULPTED SHAPE WITH A STRONG, WARM YELLOW, WHICH VISUALLY DRAWS THE FIREPLACE AWAY FROM THE COOLER WALLS AND FARTHER INTO THE ROOM. THE YELLOW ALSO CREATES A NATURAL FRAME FOR FLAMES, WHICH RADIATE RICH REDS, ORANGES, AND YELLOWS.

Left: COLOR CAN VISUALLY DELINEATE SMALLER SPACES WITHIN A LARGE, OPEN ROOM AND DENOTE TRANSITION BETWEEN AREAS. HERE, A SOFT PURPLE ARCHITECTURAL ELEMENT PROMOTES PRIVACY WITHOUT SACRIFICING THE OPEN FEEL OF THE SPACE. **Right:** ARCHITECTS CRAIG HODGETTS AND MING FUNG HIGHLIGHT A MOSTLY GLASS BEDROOM WALL WITH A SOFT WASH OF GREEN PAINT. THE TREATMENT ADDS JUST ENOUGH PROMINENCE TO THE WALL'S HORIZONTAL PROPORTIONS TO KEEP IT FROM BEING LOST BENEATH THE ROOM'S HIGH CEILINGS.

Left: A YELLOW AND GREEN PALETTE ENHANCES THE SPANISH-INSPIRED KITCHEN OF THIS 1920S CALIFORNIA BUNGALOW OWNED BY HILARY AND MICHAEL ANDERSON. THE GREEN TRIM EMPHASIZES THE VARIETY OF STRAIGHT AND ROUND ELEMENTS, HIGHLIGHTING THE ROOM'S INHERENT ARCHITECTURAL CHARACTER.

Left: THE PALETTE AND PATTERNS OF THIS DINING ROOM DESIGNED BY ARTIST ANNIE KELLY ARE A SLIGHT VARIATION ON THOSE OF THE ADJACENT LIVING ROOM, CREATING THE ILLUSION OF A ROOM WITHIN A ROOM. BLUE AND PINK BORDERS IMITATE THE LOOK OF CHAIR RAILS, AN ARCHITECTURAL DETAIL USUALLY SEEN IN MORE TRADITIONAL ROOMS THAT PROTECTS THE WALL FROM BEING SCRAPED BY CHAIR BACKS. **Right:** ALTHOUGH IT MAY APPEAR RANDOM, COLOR SHOULD NEVER BE ARBITRARILY APPLIED. HERE, COORDINATING HUES HOLD TOGETHER A CRAZY-QUILT COLLECTION OF PATTERN AND COLOR ACHIEVED THROUGH A SELECTION OF PLASTIC LAMINATES.

Above: TWO HALLWAYS SIMILAR IN THEIR DIMENSIONS ARE FEATURED SIDE BY SIDE TO ILLUSTRATE THE EXTENT TO WHICH COLOR CAN ALTER THE CHARACTER OF A SPACE. EYE-CATCHING GEOMETRY FILLS THE HALLWAY ON THE LEFT, WHICH WAS PAINTED BY ARTIST GREGORY EVANS. HIS PALETTE OF THREE CONTEMPORARY COLORS, APPLIED TO PLANES OF VARYING LENGTHS AND WIDTHS, RESHAPES THE AREA'S HORIZONTAL AND VERTICAL SPACE AND DISTINGUISHES ITS PASSAGEWAYS. THE CHOREOGRAPHED PATTERN EXTENDS TO THE FLOOR WHERE THE SAME SHADE OF RED DIVIDES AND EMPHASIZES THE SLENDER WOOD PLANKS. THE HALLWAY ON THE RIGHT, PAINTED WITH COOL BLUES AND GREENS, APPEARS TO RECEDE, CAMOUFLAGING THE WALL'S SLIGHT CURVE. **Right:** ALTHOUGH THEY ARE UNUSUAL SHADES OF YELLOW AND GREEN, THE DUET OF COLOR ON THE CHECKERBOARD WALL HARMONIZE AND FIT THE WHIMSICAL FEEL OF THIS FAMILY ROOM DESIGNED BY ARCHITECTS HANK KONING AND JULIE EIZENBERG.

Above: The palette of this family room, with interior design by Jan Turner Herring and architecture by James Kehr, is achieved through upholstery and accessories. The white walls and ceiling appear seamless, providing a neutral backdrop for the vivid accent colors. **Right:** This dining room's muted walls are the perfect background against which to showcase a collecton of colorful Riviera dinnerware.

Above: DESPITE THE MULTITUDE OF COLOR AND PATTERN IN THIS FAMILY ROOM, THE OVERALL PALETTE DOES NOT OVERWHELM; THE COMPLEMENTARY GREEN AND RED TRIM BALANCE EACH OTHER AND UNIFY THE ROOM'S COLOR SCHEME. **Left:** COLOR AND TEXTURE ENHANCE THE RICH NEUTRAL PALETTE OF THIS CRAFTSMAN-STYLE DINING ROOM BY ARCHITECT LARRY TOTAH. THE THIN BAND OF RUST-BROWN, WHICH IS COMPOSED OF HAMMERED COPPER SHEETS, REFLECTS LIGHT DIFFERENTLY FROM THE MOTTLED WALL TREATMENT LOCATED BENEATH IT (DETAIL ON PAGE 65).

PAINTED WALLS CAN BE THE PERFECT CANVAS FOR ARTWORK AND ACCESSORIES.

Right: A PEARLY OFF-WHITE IS A SUBTLE BACKDROP TO VINTAGE FURNISHINGS. SMALL AMOUNTS OF WARM YELLOWS, REDS, OR BROWNS MIXED INTO WHITE PAINT WILL CREATE A WARM, SOFT SHADE OF OFF-WHITE.

Left: A BLUE-PAINTED BRICK WALL IN THE LONDON HOME OF ARTIST ANDREW LOGAN AND ARCHITECT MICHAEL DAVIS CREATES A TEXTURED SURFACE FOR EQUALLY TEXTURED ART MIRRORS. BECAUSE THE ROOM IS OPEN TO THE SUN, THE COLORS APPEAR VIBRANT.

Right: GREEN IS SAID TO ENHANCE CONCENTRATION AND QUIET DISTRACTIONS; IT IS ALSO THOUGHT TO BE EASY TO LOOK AT AND HAVE A CALMING EFFECT. BRIGHT GREEN WORKS EXTREMELY WELL WITH BOLD YELLOWS AND GOLDS AND IS THEREFORE THE PERFECT BACKGROUND COLOR TO HIGHLIGHT THIS COLLECTION OF ANTIQUE FRAMES.

These rooms reflect a very personal, confident use of color. **Above:** An unusual combination of colors gives this bedroom a striking look. The narrow band of black on the walls and the deep blue-purple bedspread serve as a visual relief, balancing the bolder wall and ceiling colors. **Left:** The palette in Hollywood set designer Jeremy Railton's dining room is dramatic and bold, but because red, blue, and gold are prominent colors in Chinese culture and lore, it is appropriate for the oriental decor. A white ceiling helps to open up the color scheme and the room.

FOR MEXICAN ARCHITECT RICARDO LEGORRETA, COLOR AND LIGHT ARE FUNDAMENTAL DESIGN TOOLS. THIS HOME EXHIBITS HIS TRADEMARK USE OF COLOR AND ILLUSTRATES HOW IMPORTANT THE APPROPRIATE PALETTE CAN BE IN ESTABLISHING MOOD AND DISTINGUISHING ARCHITECTURE. LIMESTONE FLOORS THROUGHOUT THE HOUSE FUNCTION AS A NEUTRAL VISUAL SPRINGBOARD FOR THE EXUBERANT INTERIOR COLORS. **Left:** PAINTED LATTICE LOCATED BENEATH A SKYLIGHT WASHES DIFFUSED PINK LIGHT ON LEMON-YELLOW WALLS, CREATING A CONSTANTLY CHANGING INTERPLAY OF LIGHT, COLOR, AND SHADOW. **Above left:** AN UNUSUAL SHADE OF PURPLE FRAMES AND SHOWCASES AN EXPANSE OF GLASS IN AN INTERIOR HALLWAY. THE COLOR OF THE GLASS IS ENHANCED BY THE LAP POOL IT CONCEALS AND THE ADJACENT YELLOW WALL, WHICH MAKES THE PURPLE APPEAR RICHER AND MORE SATURATED. **Above right:** THIS EXTERIOR SAND-YELLOW CONCRETE WALL HAS LAVENDER-BLUE ACCENTS THAT MAKE IT APPEAR FLUID WHEN VIEWED FROM DIFFERENT PERSPECTIVES.

A RIOT OF COLOR PERVADES GRAPHIC DESIGNER MICK HAGGERTY'S HOME.

Above: IN KEEPING WITH THE HOME'S ABUNDANT AND VARIED USE OF COLOR, EACH SURFACE AND ARCHITECTURAL ELEMENT OF THIS BEDROOM HAS BEEN PAINTED A DIFFERENT HUE. **Above right:** A BRIGHT PALETTE TURNS AN ORDINARY PICNIC TABLE INTO DECORATIVE OUTDOOR FURNITURE AND LINKS THE TABLE TO THE HOUSE'S EXTERIOR COLOR SCHEME.

Right: TRIM PAINTED RED, PINK, YELLOW, BLUE-GREEN, AND PURPLE HUES MIMICS THE RAINBOW. **Far right:** THE SYMPHONY OF EXHILARATING COLOR PLAYS ON IN THE KITCHEN. THE ORANGE-YELLOW WALL APPEARS TO FRAME THE ARTWORK, WITH THE VISIBLE BRUSH STROKES UNDERSCORING THE FREESTYLE FEEL OF THE PICTURE.

OFF THE WALL

Nowhere is it written that paint and color belong exclusively on the walls. Walls do comprise the majority of surface area in a room, but they are by no means the only surface area. Sometimes the most dramatic color schemes come from the colorful use of other elements; consider ceilings, floors, furnishings, lighting, and accessories as much a blank canvas as a room's four walls.

As architect Brian Murphy, an independent thinker when it comes to melding design and color, is fond of saying: "You can get a lot of mileage from a dabble of color applied right." The color game is as much about ingenuity and individuality as it is about quantity.

Painted floors can expand a room's boundaries, add a refreshing decorative touch, or function as an unusual visual centerpiece. By painting surfaces and objects that are generally overlooked, an element of surprise can be brought to a color scheme. A simple gesture, planned and purposefully executed, can establish the mood and palette of an otherwise nondescript room.

Expanding the ways in which color can be added opens the door to design creativity. The photographs in this chapter present deliberate and exciting uses of color meant to inspire.

Left: In architect José de Yturbe's weekend home, potted geraniums cascade down a specially designed, stepped wall in an all-white breakfast room. The flowers' red and green palette, spotlighted by sunlight, creates a dramatic, naturally appealing color scheme. **Above:** Banana trees provide a spot of tropical color to a Hawaiian, surfer-style interior filled with unusual design gestures.

Left: IN THIS LIVING ROOM DESIGNED BY BRIAN MURPHY, CLASSIC BLACK-AND-WHITE TILES ARE A SMALL BUT STRONG FOCAL POINT THAT DRAWS THE EYE AWAY FROM THE STRIKING PURPLE WALL. **Right:** A DREAM INSPIRED MURPHY TO SUSPEND EIGHTEEN RADIANT RED CHANDELIERS FROM THE CEILING OF HIS WHITE LIVING ROOM. AFTER REMOVING THE CRYSTALS, HE PAINTED THE VARIOUS MATERIALS—METAL, PLASTIC, COPPER—A FLAT WHITE FOR A CONSISTENT BASE COLOR. HIS MONOCHRO-MATIC COLOR SCHEME UNIFIES THE MYRIAD STYLES, SHAPES, AND SIZES.

Floors comprise about one-third of a room's visual effect. Painted floors can expand the boundaries of color in the home and shape a room's character from the ground up. **Above:** Artist Annie Kelly began this decorative floor by installing plywood over existing linoleum. Next, she surrounded a monochromatic kitchen island with a sea of washed blue. The neutral border softens the transition into the adjacent rooms and further distinguishes the kitchen's unique palette. **Right:** In this charming space, a painted diamond pattern has been used to jazz up ordinary wooden floorboards. The neutral hues chosen for the design contribute to the harmony of the setting.

Above: Architect Mark Mack visually connects custom-designed wood cabinets to the surrounding room with a soft blue-gray. Interspersing bright yellow brings the mostly monochromatic wall to life, proving that a sprinkle of concentrated color can add substantial dimension and personality to a room. **Left:** A stairway, often the focal point of a multistory home, is an ideal forum for personal expression. For his own stairs, architect Barton Phelps created a palette symbolic of the wooded hill on which his home stands—deep forest-green solid vinyl flooring on the stairs and a gray-green paint on the walls. Industrial sconces, inverted and painted white, symbolize clouds. The dark-colored stairs draw the eye down and add to the feeling of descent, while the lighter walls give the illusion of rising up.

Right: EXQUISITE ARCHITECTURAL
DETAILS DESERVE DISTINCTIVE
FINISHES. THESE HAND-CRAFTED
HARDWOOD BALUSTRADES WERE
DESIGNED AND COLORED BY
MEXICAN ARCHITECT LUIS
BARRAGÁN. PAINTING ONE
SIDE OF EACH PIECE BLUE ADDS
DISTINCTION TO THE WOODWORK
AND STAIRWAY.

Right: IN THIS FAMILY ROOM DESIGNED BY MARK MACK, COLOR
ENHANCES THE ARCHITECTURE, ADDING INTEREST TO THE STAIRS, FLOOR, BOOK-
CASE, WALLS, AND FOLDING SHUTTERS.

Left: A BRIGHT PALETTE REMINISCENT OF BRAND-NEW CRAYONS COLORS A CONTEMPORARY HANDRAIL IN AN ATRIUM PLAYROOM. THIS STRUCTURE INTRODUCES A YOUTHFUL, LIGHTHEARTED SPIRIT TO THE OTHERWISE NEUTRAL PALETTE AND DANCES COLOR UP TO THE NEXT LEVEL, WHERE SIMILAR SHADES ENHANCE THE SMALL, SQUARE WINDOWS. **Right:** IN THE SAME HOME, HIGH-GLOSS PAINT COVERS BASIC WALL-HUNG BOOK-SHELVES, MAKING A BOLD STATEMENT OUT OF AN ORDINARY ARCHITECTURAL DETAIL.

Ceilings do not need to be limited to white or off-white. Other hues can create unique optical effects and change the character of a room. **Above:** Painting a ceiling a light color can make it appear higher, whereas a dark color will make it seem lower. In this room, painting the ceiling and floor the same color creates the illusion of suspended space. **Left:** In this room designed by Annie Kelly, the continuation of the ceiling color onto the top portion of the walls shrinks the vertical dimensions by making the ceiling appear lower and the walls shorter. The thin ocher band visually attaches the bottom of the room to the top.

MANY AREAS OF THE HOME ARE OVERLOOKED WHEN COLOR IS CONSIDERED. PAINTING THE INTERIOR OF A BOOKCASE OR DISPLAY CABINET CAN ADD A CONTROLLED AMOUNT OF COLOR TO LARGE OR SMALL ROOMS.

Left: THESE CUBBIES WERE CUSTOM PAINTED TO DISPLAY THE COLLECTION OF PRE-COLUMBIAN FIGURES. BLUE OFTEN DENOTES ROYALTY, AND THUS SEEMS A FITTING CHOICE FOR THE VALUABLE ARTWORK. THE SERENE UNIFORM BACKGROUND FEELS APPROPRIATE, AS MANY OF THE FIGURINES ARE DEPICTED IN CALM AND MEDITATIVE POSES. **Right:** COLOR AND DESIGN MELD PAST AND PRESENT INFLUENCES IN A REMODELED FAMILY ROOM. ARCHITECTS SCOTT JOHNSON AND MARGOT ALOFSIN PAINTED THE CUBBIES OF TWO WOOD DISPLAY CASES IN HUES THAT COMPLEMENT THE DECORATIVE GLASS AND CERAMICS THAT THEY CONTAIN. PRESENTING THE PALETTE IN A DIFFERENT PATTERN WITHIN EACH BOOKCASE ADDS VARIETY AND INTEREST WITHOUT TIPPING THE ROOM'S BALANCED DESIGN. FROM A DISTANCE, THE BOOKCASES APPEAR AS SMALL BEADS OF COLOR THAT HELP LOWER THE PERCEIVED HEIGHT OF THE CATHEDRAL CEILING.

Decorative Techniques

For centuries, artisans and craftsmen have embellished interior surfaces and furnishings with fanciful decorative paint treatments. These eye-catching techniques remain popular today for hiding or enhancing design details, taking a room to another time or place, or simply adding a touch of panache to a staid decor.

Decorative painting techniques fall into two categories. Faux (French for "false") finishes—including faux marbling, faux woodgraining, and trompe l'oeil (meaning "to fool the eye")—mimic a real material or object. Trompe l'oeil is a particularly captivating technique that creates realistic focal points or vistas through a freehand application or the use of stencils. Marbling and woodgraining are ideal for simulating sumptuous surfaces without the expense of costly building materials.

The second category of decorative painting techniques includes treatments that do not simulate but simply adorn. Perhaps the most popular and easily achieved treatments are stenciling and colorwashing, which add flourish and a homemade feel to surfaces and furnishings. Stenciling is considered one of the most versatile painting techniques and is certainly one of the easiest ways to add a decorative border or pattern to a painted surface. Colorwashing walls or furniture—applying a diluted color to a neutral base coat with rags, sponges, or brushes—gives them a brushy, cloudlike appearance and is particularly popular in country interiors.

These are by no means the only techniques available. As the following photos attest, there is no limit to what can be accomplished with paint, color, and an artistic eye.

Left: Walls and canvas screens painted with trompe l'oeil by artist Julian Latrobe encircle a classical interior designed by Hutton Wilkinson. The illusionary landscape turns the elegant living room into a Roman temple at sunset. The off-white and golden hues look exceptionally warm when gently lighted at night. **Above, left and right:** Trompe l'oeil book spines conceal shelf-size speakers in the home of the late master lyricist Ira Gershwin. Actual books were copied in detail, down to the publisher and author.

Left: A COMBINATION OF DECORATIVE PAINT TECHNIQUES—STENCILING, COLORWASHING, FREEHAND DESIGN, AND TROMPE L'OEIL—EPITOMIZES THE CREATIVE POWER OF PAINT AND COLOR. DOORS BECOME WHIMSICAL PORTRAITS, AND WALLS TURN INTO SHIMMERING FRAMES. **Right:** A TECHNIQUE KNOWN AS FAUX MARBLING, WHICH IMITATES THE LUXURIOUS LOOK OF MARBLE, CARVES OUT A STUNNING FIREPLACE IN COLORS NEW TO MOTHER NATURE'S QUARRIES. THE IMAGINATIVE SWIRLING AND RICH COLORS ADD TEXTURE AND DRAMA TO THE FIREPLACE, MAKING IT A FOCAL POINT FOR DECORATIVE ACCESSORIES AND FURNISHINGS. ARTIST STEVE SHRIVER'S ARTFUL SHADING OF THE GOLD-PAINTED ACCENTS ON THE MANTEL GIVES THE ILLUSION OF DIMENSION.

Below: TROMPE L'OEIL CAN BE USED TO TRANSFORM AN ARCHITECTURAL ELEMENT INTO SOMETHING SPECIAL. HERE, AN ORDINARY PANTRY DOOR IS DISGUISED AS A WINDOW TO THE OUTSIDE, DISPLAYING FARMLAND AND A COW PEERING CURIOUSLY INSIDE.

Left: ELSIE DEWOLFE, A PIONEER IN THE INTERIOR DESIGN FIELD, PRODUCED THIS ORNATE CUSTOM SECRETARY. THE DARK GREEN INTERIOR CUBBIES RESEMBLE TINY, PLUSH JEWEL BOXES DISPLAYING THEIR PRECIOUS CONTENTS. INTRICATE STENCILING EMBELLISHES THE PANELS. PLACED AGAINST A COLORWASHED WALL, THE CABINET APPEARS EVEN MORE FANCIFUL. **Above:** ANNIE KELLY'S STUDIO FEATURES A HAND-PAINTED WALL AND A CUBIST-INSPIRED, HAND-PAINTED CABINET. CLASSIC STRIPES OF VIVID YELLOW AND WHITE CREATE AN OUTDOOR, SUNNY FEELING THAT PLAYS AGAINST THE CABINET'S BLUE-GRAY MURAL.

Left: A CUSTOM HAND-PAINTED CHINA HUTCH CHEERS UP A MEXICAN VERANDA WITH COLORS AND PATTERNS REMINISCENT OF MEXICAN TEXTILES AND POTTERY.

Right: SIMPLE, UNPRETENTIOUS FINISHES ON WOOD FURNISHINGS COMPLEMENT COUNTRY AND RUSTIC INTERIORS. THE DELIBERATE CHIPPING AWAY OF PAINT ADDS TEXTURE AND A SENSE OF AGELESSNESS TO THIS OLD CABINET. THE BRUSHY BLUE WASH COVERING THE WALL IS A SOFT AND GENTLE BACKGROUND FOR THE ROOM'S OPEN, AIRY FEELING.

Right: THERE IS NO REASON WHY DECORATIVE PAINT TECHNIQUES SHOULD STAY BEHIND CLOSED DOORS. HERE, A TROMPE L'OEIL THROW RUG DRAPES GARDEN STAIRS AT THE ACAPULCO HOME OF MEXICAN ARCHITECT MARCO ALDACO. KEEPING THE RISERS FAIRLY PLAIN AND RESTRICTING THE HAND-PAINTED PATTERN TO THE TREADS MAKES THE IMAGINARY CARPET APPEAR MORE REALISTIC.

Below: THE RIGHT COLOR AND PAINT TREATMENT CAN HELP MASK A ROUGH SURFACE; A DELICATE PINK WASH SOFTENS THIS CONCRETE FIREPLACE.

Right: ARCHITECT LARRY TOTAH WASHED A PLASTER WALL WITH MURATIC ACID, SCRAPED AWAY THE EXISTING PAINT, AND VEILED THE WALL—SINCE DIMPLED FROM THE ACID—WITH DILUTED WATER-BASE PAINTS. ALTHOUGH THE TREATMENT BEGAN AS AN EXPERIMENT, THE RESULT APPEARS WELL THOUGHT-OUT (OVERVIEW ON PAGE 30). THE CHAIR WAS DESIGNED BY JON BOK.

EXTERIORS

A home's exterior gives the first impression of its contents. The shape, color, and texture of exterior surfaces and design elements can say as much about a home as its interior architecture and palette. The selection of a color scheme for the outside of a house should be as deliberate as it is for the interior palette.

Exterior colors can be chosen for their ability to link a home to its surroundings or architectural history. The palette might evoke a regional heritage or be compatible with nearby landscapes. For a house that has been remodeled, exterior paint might be chosen to connect the original structure to or distinguish it from the addition. As they do on the inside, paint and color on the exterior can change the perception of a home's overall size and proportions, highlight certain aspects of the architecture, or make allusions to a bygone era. And paint and color used outside of the home can add a sense of design where it's least expected, such as to a fence or roof.

When choosing color for outdoor surfaces, it's important to consider the impact of daily and seasonally changing light. The sun produces intense light in areas close to the equator; in areas farther away, especially in winter months, it is more muted and gray. The texture of building materials can also alter the perception of color due to the interplay of light and shadow. Fortunately, many of today's paints are formulated to preserve color against the elements, so aesthetics can take priority.

The homes and exterior features on the following pages represent a range of palettes and applications, illustrating how colors look on expansive surfaces, how paint influences architecture, and above all, why the choice of exterior color should be made thoughtfully.

Left: EXTENDING AN INTERIOR COLOR TO AN EXTERIOR ENTRANCE SMOOTHS THE TRANSITION BETWEEN INDOOR AND OUTDOOR SPACES. CARRYING THE SAME COLOR TO THE CEILING ON EITHER SIDE OF THE DOOR GIVES THE EFFECT OF SEAMLESS CONSTRUCTION. **Above:** TIME AND WEATHER IMPACT EXTERIOR COLORS, SOMETIMES WITH WONDERFUL EFFECTS. THE FADED SALMON FACADE OF ARCHITECT BRIAN MURPHY'S HOME IS ACTUALLY THE RESULT OF DECADES OF WEATHERING. COOL YELLOW- AND BLUE-PAINTED WINDOW SASHES, A REFRESHING VISUAL BREAK, PUNCTUATE THE EXTERIOR OF THE HOUSE.

EXTERIOR PALETTES CAN BE AS VIVID AND IMAGINATIVE AS INTERIOR ONES. **Above:** ARTIST PETER SHIRE

APPLIES HIS EYE FOR COLOR TO HIS FORMER TRACT HOME IN LOS ANGELES. THE STRONG TROPICAL COLORS HE HAS CHOSEN

REMAIN VIBRANT IN THE BRIGHT CALIFORNIA SUNLIGHT. **Right:** ARCHITECTS CRAIG HODGETTS AND MING

FUNG USE A CONTEMPORARY PALETTE TO COMPLEMENT THE STRUCTURE AND DESIGN OF THIS MODERN HILLSIDE HOME.

Left: MANY VICTORIAN HOMES ARE AS MEMORABLE FOR THEIR INTERPLAY OF COLOR AND ARCHITECTURE AS FOR THEIR DISTINCTIVE SHAPES. THIS HOME IS ASPEN, COLORADO, IS NO EXCEPTION. TOUCHES OF YELLOW, SHADES OF VIOLET, AND BRIGHT WHITE EMPHASIZE TRIM AND OTHER DECORATIVE DETAILS.

Left: IN AN IRONIC STATEMENT, THE PALETTE CHOSEN FOR THIS FUNKY DESERT HOUSE DESIGNED BY ARCHITECT JOSH SCHWEITZER SYMBOLIZES THE BASIC COLORS FOUND IN NATURE: THE POWDER-BLUE BUILDING REPRESENTS THE SKY, THE YELLOW CHIMNEY EVOKES THE SUN, THE GREEN CENTER STRUCTURE SUGGESTS GRASS, AND THE SMALL ORANGE BUILDING MIMICS THE COLOR OF CLAY FOUND IN DESERTS AND DRY ENVIRONMENTS.

Left: MEXICAN LORE HOLDS THAT CERTAIN COLORS WARD OFF EVIL SPIRITS, AND FOR THIS REASON THEY ARE TRADITIONALLY USED INSIDE THE HOME. THIS SOLID-LOOKING BACK-YARD WALL PAINTED A COLOR CALLED AZUL AÑIL FUNCTIONS AS AN AMULET PROTECTING A MEXICAN HOME. CONTRASTING VERTICAL RED BANDS REINFORCE THE GARDEN WALL'S FORMIDABLE APPEARANCE.

Right: THE BLUE COLOR OF THIS PIGMENTED PLASTER WALL WAS CARE-FULLY MIXED TO APPROXIMATE AS CLOSELY AS POSSIBLE THE COLOR OF THE POOL BEYOND. THE WALL SEPA-RATES THE ENTRANCE COURT OF THIS HOME DESIGNED BY FRANKLIN D. ISRAEL FROM THE PRIVATE BACKYARD, AND LIKE WORN BLUE JEANS, FADES PLEASANTLY OVER TIME.

Below: A COLORFUL ROOF CAN SET A HOME APART FROM OR, AS SHOWN HERE, HELP IT MELD WITH THE ENVIRONMENT. THE COLLECTION OF HUES IN THIS PATTERNED, MULTICOLORED TILE ROOF ALLOWS THE HOME TO BLEND WITH THE SURROUNDING SAND AND PALM TREES.

Above: THE PERVASIVE USE OF A WARM SHADE OF GREEN TURNS AN ORDINARY GARDEN TRELLIS INTO LANDSCAPE ARCHITECTURE OUTSIDE THIS HOME DESIGNED BY MARK MACK. SHADING THE SUN DECK A MATCHING GREEN UNIFIES THE HOUSE AND GARDEN.

Left and below: THESE TWO HOMES LOOK LIKE NEGATIVES OF ONE ANOTHER. GREEN IS USED AS AN ACCENT COLOR ON THE HOUSE BELOW, RESEMBLING ICING PIPED ONTO A CAKE AND CALLING ATTENTION TO THE HOME'S DISTINCTIVE LINES AND ANGLES. GREEN IS THE PREDOMINANT COLOR OF THE HOUSE ON THE LEFT, WITH WHITE EMPHASIZING THE DETAILING OF THE WOODWORK AND ROOF.

Left: GREEN IS A NATURAL CHOICE FOR BLENDING HOMES WITH LUSH FOLIAGE. HERE, THE EYE IS DRAWN NATURALLY FROM THE DARK GREEN OF THE HOUSE TO THE SURROUNDING LANDSCAPE. THE WHITE SURFACES ARE A REFRESHING INTERLUDE FROM THE MANY SHADES OF GREEN.

Above: ARCHITECT FRANKLIN D. ISRAEL DESIGNED A SERIES OF INTERCONNECTED PAVILIONS FOR THE REMODELING OF THIS HOME, WITH COLOR SIGNALING A CHANGE OR VARIATION IN THE ARCHITECTURE. THE PALETTE REPRESENTS THE THREE PRIMARY COLORS; MUSTARD-YELLOW PLASTER SURFACES, REDWOOD-STAINED CEDAR, AND A BLUE GARDEN WALL. **Right:** A PATIO WITH AN OUTDOOR FIREPLACE EVOKES THE FEELING OF AN OPEN-AIR LIVING ROOM. ARCHITECT JEFFREY TOHL HAD THE PLASTER AND WOOD FEATURES PAINTED THE SAME RICH TERRA COTTA COLOR, BLURRING THE BOUNDARIES BETWEEN THE DIFFERENT SURFACES AND TEXTURES. THE EARTHY HUE ALSO PROVIDES A NATURAL COMPLEMENT TO THE GREEN GRASS.

Left: MOTHER NATURE IS THE CONSUMMATE COLORIST, FOREVER COMBINING COLORS INTO BREATHTAKING, CAPTIVATING PALETTES. A SHIMMERING SUNSET IN CAREYES, MEXICO, IS FILLED WITH HUES OF PINK, BLUE, YELLOW, AND VIOLET. THE PASTEL COLORS INSPIRED ARCHITECT MARCO ALDECO TO WASH A RESIDENTIAL ROOFTOP IN COOL HUES OF BLUE AND PURPLE. THE STARK-WHITE EDGE ABRUPTLY DIVIDES THE VISTA AND CLEANSES THE EYE IN PREPARATION FOR THE COLORFUL, DYNAMIC HORIZON BEYOND.

PART TWO

NATURAL COLOR PALETTES

INTRODUCTION

IN ALL THINGS OF NATURE THERE IS SOMETHING OF THE MARVELOUS.

—Aristotle (384–322 B.C.E.)

Marvelous indeed—especially when it comes to color. Consider for just a moment how the words "natural color palette" immediately bring to mind the great outdoors. Standing in a field of wildflowers, we are mesmerized by the combination of both vibrant and soft hues. Gazing at a winter landscape, we're overcome by the spirit of beauty played out in subtle whites and grays. Or, strolling on an autumn day, we can be riveted by the display of leaves changing from green to russet and gold.

Take a good look around you. Notice the peaceful blue of a cloudless sky or the more intense color of a churning sea. Pay attention to how light seems to alter natural colors as the hours of the day go by—white clouds can turn to pink, deep red, or lavender during a sunset. It's no wonder we long to bring such colors inside and surround ourselves with a palette that evokes tranquility and a sense of well-being.

Natural colors, inspired by nature and created using natural elements, have a long history of use in interior design. Early homes had rugged walls constructed of logs, stone, or clay. Bricks and tiles were later used for functional as well as decorative purposes. These earthy substances were joined by other natural materials, such as linen, cotton, silk, and muslin, that were used on furnishings and for window dressings. Colorful decorative accents, reminiscent of the select shades found in nature, were created with natural dyes and minerals to add a cheerful note to both rural and urban homes.

Opposite: IN THIS ELEGANT LIVING ROOM, WALLPAPER SPORTING STRIPES OF TAUPE AND WHITE PLAYS HOST TO UPHOLSTERED PIECES BEARING SIMILAR HUES. A LOVELY BROWN AREA RUG, BEARING SWIRLS OF SANDY BEIGE, SITS ATOP NATURAL FIBER MATTING TO DEFINE THE CONVERSATION AREA. OTHER ELEMENTS THAT PAY HOMAGE TO NATURE COME INTO PLAY, INCLUDING NUMEROUS LEAFY PATTERNS AND TWO DECORATIVE TABLE LAMPS (ONE SPORTING A PAINTED PALM TREE, THE OTHER SPROUTING GILDED LEAVES). AS A RESULT, THE ROOM VIVIDLY RECALLS THE OUTDOORS WHILE PROVIDING ALL THE CREATURE COMFORTS OF HOME.

Above: OFF-WHITE WALLS AND COORDINATING WINDOW SHADES FASHION A DISTRACTION-FREE BACKDROP IN THIS CONTEMPORARY WORK SPACE. THE NON-FUSSY WINDOW TREATMENT AND THE PALE, SMOOTH SURFACES OF THE MODERN DESK AND BENCH NOT ONLY BLEND EFFORTLESSLY TO ESTABLISH A NEUTRAL COLOR SCHEME, BUT ALSO WORK TOGETHER TO GIVE THE AREA A SLEEK LOOK.

During the eighteenth century, interiors often bore neutral color schemes, with gray, buff, and various shades of white being the simplest hues to create. Terra-cotta and umber were made from clay, while certain vegetables and flowers were called upon to make dyes that would transform homespun fabrics into a kaleidoscope of deep or softly faded hues. For example, cranberries were used to turn fabric red, while ragweed flowers or iris petals were employed to concoct a lovely shade of green. Minerals, too, were an important ingredient in early dyes—blue was derived from lapis lazuli and green from malachite.

By the late nineteenth century, synthetic dyes had been developed, thereby expanding the color choices available for home decor. The Victorians made wonderful use of color in their eclectic, sometimes shocking interiors. With the exception of the Arts and Crafts Movement (which called for the use of natural dyes in printed fabric), interior design progressed steadily into the twentieth century with a bright new focus on the development of color, courtesy of advances in technology that presented new possibilities for decorating the home.

Trends and styles may come and go, but one constant seems to be a deeply rooted desire for peaceful retreats from the outside world. Today, this still translates into rooms that echo the beauty of nature.

How, then, do you go about selecting a natural color palette for your own home? Colors you find yourself drawn to again and again often form a basis from which to start. Blue is regarded as an all-time favorite, with green usually running a close second. No matter what your preference, the almost limitless variations available can seem overwhelming. However, they can be narrowed down by keeping some key points in mind.

As discussed in Part One, when it comes to "talking the talk," most colors are considered to be either "warm" or "cool." And they are linked to certain emotions or moods. Warm colors include vibrant reds, oranges, and yellows, as well as such lighter tints as pink and apricot. Since warm colors are energizing and stimulating, they often prove ideal in rooms with limited natural lighting. This sensation of vitality also makes these colors appropriate for high-activity rooms: picture a yellow kitchen or a deep red dining room. And let's not forget the home office, where a warm color can help increase productivity.

In contrast, cool colors, such as blues and greens, are calming, infusing the rooms they adorn with serenity. These hues are shown off to their best advantage in areas with an abundance of natural light. When selecting a natural palette for a small room, keep in mind that cool colors will make the space appear larger. These relaxing hues are often favored for the bedroom (where quiet repose is ideal), library, and bath, the latter being increasingly viewed as a pleasure/relaxation room more than a strictly utilitarian space.

Choosing a natural color palette for any given room may be as simple as building around a favorite rug, a

Above: WE USUALLY THINK OF BEDROOMS IN TERMS OF COOL COLORS, BUT WARM HUES CAN BE TONED DOWN TO CREATE A SOOTHING PALETTE. HERE, A SPECIAL PAINTING TECHNIQUE GIVES THE OCHER WALLS AND CEILING A FADED LOOK THAT CREATES A RELAXING AMBIENCE. POPPY-COLORED BEDDING RAISES THE TEMPERATURE SLIGHTLY, BUT THIS EFFECT IS TEMPERED BY THE LOW-KEY DEMEANOR OF THE PAINT-CHIPPED WROUGHT-IRON BED FRAME.

Above: SINCE THIS TRADITIONAL DINING ROOM HAS A PRIMARILY NEUTRAL BACKDROP, THE DARK GREEN PLATES DISPLAYED ON THE HUTCH REALLY STAND OUT AND SERVE AS THE SPACE'S FOCAL POINT. MORE SUBTLE TOUCHES OF GREEN APPEAR IN THE CANDLES, AREA RUG, AND STENCILED BORDERS RUNNING ALONGSIDE THE CHAIR RAIL AND CORNICE. OFTENTIMES, THE RESTRAINED USE OF A DEEP SHADE CREATES THE PERFECT MEASURE OF VISUAL IMPACT.

treasured painting, or a piece of furniture. Inspiration may come from the view outside your window or the longing to re-create the ambience of a woodland cottage or a seaside retreat. No matter where the idea originates, selecting specific colors will be easier if you know the difference between a "shade" and a "tint," and understand the concept of "tone." A shade is developed by adding black to a specific color, while a tint is the end result after adding white. We often refer to pastels as tints and muted colors as shades. Tone simply refers to the depth of color (how light or dark) and applies to both tints and shades.

Regardless of your decorative style, almost any natural palette can be incorporated. Remember that walls are not the only elements to consider when establishing the color scheme. The beauty of the outdoors can be reflected in flooring, the ceiling, window dressings, furnishings, and decorative accessories. Upholstery, carpeting, drapes, and treasured objects all come into play. As with any chosen palette, natural colors can be used to define different spaces or to cause one room to flow smoothly into another. Color is also an excellent means of drawing attention to architectural embellishments, such as moldings, mantels, and built-in bookcases.

Naturally, once you decide upon a color scheme, you'll want to achieve pleasing, long-lasting results. In regard to paint, satin finishes (having a slight sheen) are ideal for living rooms, bedrooms, and dining rooms, where

Left: Here, a pastel color scheme is used to join two rooms that flow into each other, creating a unified master suite. Since the bedroom and spalike bathroom are highly visible from each other, even when the pocket doors fitted with etched glass are closed, it is important that the decors be integrated deftly. Thus, different pastels that go hand in hand were selected, establishing a decorative whole, while at the same time giving each space its own subtle air of distinction. Notice how the pink flowers painted on the bathroom wall pick up the predominant color of the bedroom.

occasional wiping with a damp sponge may be required. For hard-working rooms, such as the kitchen and bath, and for woodwork that tends to accumulate fingerprints, a semigloss paint will facilitate cleaning. Flat paints can be used on ceilings and in low traffic areas where smudges are unlikely.

The chapters that follow examine specific natural color palettes and present a plethora of inspiring ideas for bringing the colors you love to the rooms you live in. Never underestimate the power of natural colors—they can transform an ordinary home into the most extraordinary and inviting of settings.

Soft Neutrals

Several of the beautiful colors found in nature are what we refer to as neutral hues. Variations of cream, beige, sand, and taupe, as well as the numerous whites, allow for versatile, timeless, and soothing interiors. And let's not forget gray, which can present a calming, subtle backdrop. These natural colors have the powerful ability to recall such scenes as a sparkling, crisp winter day, a striking desert landscape, or a peaceful ocean beach, where light dances and plays with the hues of smooth pebbles and sandy stretches.

Neutral colors have been used in various dwellings for ages. White, which has long been associated with cleanliness, was symbolic of a joyful home in ancient times. Gray, meanwhile, has historically been linked to spirituality and religious ceremonies. The various shades and tints of brown impart elegance, old-world charm, and even a simple rusticity.

While neutrals can certainly stand alone, they also boast the ability to live harmoniously with stronger colors. Highly versatile, neutral hues work well with contemporary and traditional decors. They often provide the backdrop in Scandinavian country–style rooms and lend an air of sophistication to interiors decorated in American country style.

Neutral colors are frequently chosen for monochromatic schemes that incorporate various tints and shades of a single hue. When a monochromatic or related color scheme is used in a setting, texture becomes an important means of maintaining visual interest. For example, wood flooring, lace curtains, wicker furniture, and such accessories as baskets and flowers can all bear similar hues, yet at the same time provide a sense of variety that will enhance the decorative picture. Architectural details, such as moldings, can also pitch in to add another dimension.

Opposite: TAUPE WALLS ARE ACCOMPANIED BY ACCENTS OF WHITE—IN THE ARCHITECTURAL TRIM, BUILT-IN BOOKCASES, AND WOOD-BEAMED VAULTED CEILING—TO HELP KEEP THIS SUBDUED SETTING UPLIFTING. AIRY CURTAINS THAT ADMIT PLENTY OF NATURAL LIGHT ALSO HELP TO BRIGHTEN UP THE SPACE. BY LEAVING THE HARDWOOD FLOOR BARE, THE OWNER HAS ACHIEVED A REFINED YET NATURAL LOOK THAT WARMS UP THE ROOM.

Neutral colors can, of course, team up with bolder shades, and there are certain pairings that work particularly well. White, of course, goes with everything, whether it makes up the backdrop or manifests itself as the predominant color. Cream works quite nicely with greens and blues, while gray makes a handsome companion for pink. And sand and beige are flattered by black, dark blue, or a softer pale blue.

Obviously, your walls offer the largest canvases when it comes to color. Paint is the most cost-effective and flexible choice for a wall treatment, and there are even textured paints that provide an extra dimension. However, you are by no means restricted to paint; myriad options await beyond this realm. A monochromatic wallpaper with a subtle design (stripes perhaps), beadboard wainscoting painted a soft white, and pale wood paneling are but a few of the possibilities for heightening a room's charisma. When mulling over your options, think about the mood that each wall treatment evokes. Does something with a casual feel or a more formal air best suit your style?

When it comes to flooring, neutral colors are naturals. Hardwood, plank, painted, and parquet flooring all lend themselves to a neutral color scheme. In addition, carpeting—especially something with a notable texture such as a Berber rug—will help keep the decor engaging. Stone flooring can introduce such hues as pale gray, beige, or buff, while the vast world of tile offers a never-ending array of demeanors and practical benefits. For added comfort and color underfoot, an Oriental area rug can supply a fitting decorative touch. Other welcome coverings include nubby rag rugs and area rugs composed of such natural fibers as sisal, coir, jute, and sea grass. Made from plants grown in South America, Africa, or Asia, natural fiber rugs are available in different sizes and are often accessorized with decorative bindings. Sisal rugs, the most popular of the natural fiber species, are durable and can be dyed different colors. One word of caution, however: natural fiber rugs can be difficult to clean and will show stains. With this in mind, it's probably best to reserve them for select rooms that don't have a lot of traffic or opt for wool carpeting that has the look of sisal.

For window dressings, think airy lace curtains, patterned or textured sheers, wood shutters, fabric blinds, cotton curtains, bamboo shades, or stunning drapes made of silk or brocade. Clear indicators of a relaxed or formal tone, window treatments contribute an abundance of decorative style. For example, lace lends a gentle touch of romance and cottage charm, while a layered treatment speaks of opulence. Fabric shades can go contemporary, while shutters can imbue a room with simple rustic appeal.

Furnishings, which above all should be comfortable, can be accented with strong textures, such as wicker or wood. Depending upon your personal style, your rooms may call for refined pieces or a casual, plump sofa and cozy easy chairs that invite curling up. Upholstery in neutral hues is available in a wide range of materials and patterns. Slipcovers, too, lend easy elegance in a soft white or beige.

Finishing touches include everything from artwork and favorite collections to woven throws and toss pillows to such natural elements as green plants, baskets, and seashells. Also consider adding black accents (in lamp bases or frames), a display of vintage creamware, or glassware in nature-inspired colors. With a neutral palette, it's easy to change your decorative accessories to reflect the change in the seasons—such subtle variations can breathe new life into your favorite rooms on a fairly regular basis.

Last, but certainly not least, neutral colors can be highly successful in the kitchen and bath. Wood cabinetry—especially pale wood tones—and painted-white cabinetry will blend beautifully with modern appliances and fixtures. Consider using such decorative elements as tile in a neutral or bolder shade (for accent) or with a hand-painted design to create a signature touch. Appliances, available in a wide range of colors including white, black, and sand, are a snap to coordinate with a neutral color scheme.

Above: PUNCTUATING A WHITE BACKGROUND WITH OTHER NEUTRAL COLORS ACHIEVES A SUBTLY REFINED LOOK, AS EVIDENCED BY THIS LIVING ROOM. SAND-COLORED CUSHIONS ON THE WINDOW SEAT PROMISE THE PEACEFUL REPOSE OF RELAXING ON THE BEACH. MEANWHILE, BLACK ACCENTS—IN THE CHAIR AND PICTURE FRAMES—ADD A SOPHISTICATED FLAIR. NOTE, TOO, THE BEAUTIFUL, NATURAL TEXTURES OF THE STONE HEARTH AND LUSH GREEN PLANTS.

Right: HERE, NATURAL ELEMENTS MAKE UP A NEUTRAL PALETTE. WALLS OF HORIZONTAL PLANKING AND A TONGUE-AND-GROOVE CEILING, BOTH OF WHICH ARE LEFT UNPAINTED TO LET THEIR NATURAL GRAINING SHINE, GIVE THIS HOME A CASUAL FEEL. THE RUSTIC MOOD IS AUGMENTED BY EARTHY TERRA-COTTA FLOOR TILES, WARM WOODEN FURNISHINGS, AND A NAVAJO RUG. A LARGE SUPPLY OF LOGS, NESTLED SNUGLY INTO THE SIDE OF A STONE FIREPLACE, ENHANCES THE NATURAL LOOK AND PROMISES THAT A COMFORTING FIRE CAN BE HAD AT A MOMENT'S NOTICE.

Above: Various shades of white have been used in tandem to fashion a tranquil and inviting living room.

Though painted in the same hue as the rest of the walls, chair rails pop out to prevent these surfaces from seeming too bland.

Meanwhile, blond wooden furnishings add another touch of variety, yet maintain the creamy look. Plump pillows and potted palms

heighten the alluring nature of this room, where comfort is of the utmost importance.

Above: PALE WOOD TONES GIVE THIS CONTEMPORARY DINING ROOM A CLEAN, STREAMLINED APPEARANCE. IN THE ADJOINING LIVING ROOM, SLIDING GLASS DOORS AND A VAST SKYLIGHT ENHANCE THE REFRESHING LOOK BY USHERING IN SUNLIGHT AND BRINGING NATURE INDOORS. NATURE IS FURTHER INCORPORATED INTO THE DECOR BY THE CHAIR UPHOLSTERY, WHICH FEATURES A SWIRLING VINE DESIGN THAT PICKS UP THE BLOND TONES OF THE TABLE AND FLOOR.

Opposite: A CONTEMPORARY SPACE IS INFUSED WITH ELEGANCE, COURTESY OF LINEN-COLORED WALLS, STRONG TEXTURES, AND PROMINENT ACCENT COLORS. THE FOCAL POINT IS AN ORNAMENTAL SCREEN THAT COMMANDS ATTENTION WITH ITS BOLD PATTERN AND POWERFUL SPLASHES OF BROWN AND BLACK, YET LINKS ITSELF TO THE SETTING BY SPORTING TOUCHES OF THE HUE THAT GRACES THE WALLS. THE COMBINATION OF THE DARK WOOD TABLE AND WHITE UPHOLSTERY PROVIDES SIMILAR CONTRAST.

Above: Dressed completely in white and draped with a gauzy canopy, this bed creates the sensation of floating on a cloud. Cherubs fluttering above the mirror enhance the heavenly feeling, while natural fiber rugs paired with a gray and white marble floor create the illusion of a stormy sea and patches of dry land below. The overall feeling is one of coziness and security.

Left: TAUPE AND WHITE MAKE A STUNNING DUO IN THIS BEDROOM RETREAT. THE ARCHITECTURAL MOLDING AND THE BEAMED CEILING ARE SPOTLIGHTED BY WHITE PAINT THAT PROVIDES CONTRAST AGAINST THE WALLS. A GRAY METAL CABINET SERVES AS A NOVEL BEDSIDE TABLE, WHILE THE BLACK BED SPORTS SMOOTH WHITE LINENS. PROVIDING THE PERFECT FINISHING TOUCH, A BLACK-AND-WHITE PHOTOGRAPH OF A LANDSCAPE HANGS NEXT TO THE BED.

Opposite: Thanks to the treatment of the coffered ceiling, this kitchen is completely enveloped in a natural color palette. By painting each section a slightly different shade, the owners have created a highly engaging display that flows down to the upper portion of the walls. The dividing white trim, which echoes the cabinetry, calls attention to the ceiling, while recessed lighting performs its service without detracting from the design.

Above: This state-of-the-art kitchen features a neutral color scheme for a clean, smart look. Pale wood cabinetry and a tile floor bearing variations of gray and beige are brought to life by the black countertop and seating at the island. Tiles that echo the hue of the cabinetry join ones in a deeper brown to form an eye-catching backsplash that becomes an instant focal point.

Opposite: PALE, CREAMY TILES, A STONE VANITY WITH SUBTLE COLOR VARIATIONS, AND A SIMILARLY HUED STONE BASIN IMBUE THIS BATHROOM WITH THE SERENITY OF A SPA. A GLEAMING METAL-FRAMED MIRROR AND A TRIO OF SILVER BUD VASES ADD A TOUCH OF ELEGANCE TO THE SCENE, WHICH BRINGS TO MIND THE WHITE SANDS OF GREECE.

Above: A WHITE PEDESTAL SINK AND A PALE WOOD VANITY GIVE THIS ROOM A SLIGHTLY SCANDINAVIAN FEEL. BEIGE WALLS AND WHITE TRIM ESTABLISH A QUIET BACKDROP THAT IS WARMED BY TILE FLOORING AND GREENERY. TOGETHER, THESE ELEMENTS CREATE A CASUAL ATMOSPHERE—PERFECT FOR A LONG SOAK IN THE TUB. **Right:** A SIMPLE DECOR CAN INDEED BE QUITE STRIKING WHEN DECKED IN NEUTRAL COLORS. WHITE WALLS AND NATURAL FIBER CARPETING ARE PUNCTUATED BY A BLACK CLAW-FOOT TUB AND DELICATE-LOOKING METAL SHELVING THAT HOLDS A GENEROUS SUPPLY OF PLUSH, WHITE TOWELS. THANKS TO THE CONTINUATION OF THE COLOR SCHEME INTO THE BEDROOM, WHICH IS VISIBLE THROUGH THE ARCH, ONE ROOM FLOWS SMOOTHLY INTO THE NEXT.

Subtle Pastels

Pastels, those soft colors reminiscent of a spring day, can be used to create breathtaking rooms. Especially at home in settings with an abundance of natural light, pastels in either warm or cool hues can metamorphose a small space into one that seems airy and expansive. Pale blue, which has long been associated with happiness, will set a soothing tone, while a soft pink will liven up a bath, especially when combined with shiny white fixtures. A light and creamy yellow, symbolic of intellectual growth, is often favored for kitchens because of its fresh and cheerful demeanor. And apricot, pale peach, or even a mint green can transform a living room into an inviting family retreat. The options are almost limitless.

Pastel colors are created by mixing white with a primary or secondary color; for instance, pink is a mixture of white and red. These hues first became fashionable during the eighteenth century in France, where rococo bedchambers were transformed with soft tints that added a whole new dimension. Pastels have been popular ever since, particularly with those who see nature in these charming hues and long to bring a gentle hint of the outdoors inside. Just savoring the beauty of a flower garden reveals nature-created pastel colors—the pink rose, the pale yellow daffodil, the soft blue of Jacob's ladder. Due to their light tone, pastels have long been considered feminine colors. Pink, often viewed as the most feminine of them all, is symbolic of love and romance, as is its primary component—red.

White trim and accents are ideal for keeping sprightly pastels in line and preventing them from overwhelming a space. Other colors, such as muted shades and jewel tones, also coordinate pleasantly with pastels, creating interesting visual dynamics. A perfect example is a complementary color scheme (one that includes any two opposing colors on the color wheel). Pink can be joined by a deep green, or a pale yellow can be enhanced with a

Opposite: IN THIS LIGHT AND AIRY SETTING, PASTELS ARE INTRODUCED THROUGH A TILED FIREPLACE SURROUND. THE WARM PINK AND APRICOT HUES MATCH THE WARMTH OF THE PINE FLOOR. TOSS PILLOWS IN SIMILAR HUES, WITH SOME BLUE AND GREEN ACCENTS, CONTRIBUTE TO THE OVERALL APPEAL.

royal blue. Neutral colors, especially in the form of rugs or furnishings, can also be blended into a pastel palette with great success.

If you intend to paint walls in a pastel hue, select a paint with a flat or satin finish to avoid creating an intense sheen. By incorporating white trim, you can make architectural elements, such as cornices, picture rails, chair rails, and built-in bookcases, more pronounced. The same effect can be achieved by using a deeper pastel for these details.

When it comes to wallpaper, perpetual favorites are mini prints, stripes, and floral designs; these are generally linked to cottage, country, or Victorian Revival decors. However, pastel wallpapers can be used successfully in contemporary settings, rooms with an Art Deco flair, and Scandinavian interiors, as well.

Flooring options for a pastel color scheme range from hardwoods and planking to carpeting, tile, and decorative rugs. Pastels work wonderfully with the warmer wood tones found in such popular woods as oak and honey pine. Terra-cotta tiles, whose orangy hues cast a soft glow on the surroundings, make an agreeable match for pink or apricot walls. And a faded Oriental rug bearing cool jewel tones will deftly enhance a pale blue or mint green backdrop.

Faded fabrics, as well as ones deliberately "aged" (soaked in tea), often go hand in hand with pastel colors. Florals and stripes are among the obvious choices, but since there are no hard-and-fast rules, select upholstery and drapes that successfully convey your personal style. Plump sofas and easy chairs, wicker painted white, faux-bamboo tables, and rosewood or mahogany furnishings are perfect for a cottage decor, while black accents, cream trim, and chrome tables recall Art Deco styling.

Windows dressed in lace, bamboo shades, chintz curtains, or luxurious silk drapes are but a few possibilities when working with a pastel color scheme. Lace, available in white or "natural," has the advantage of adding both texture and pattern. Plus, its delicate nature makes it a highly suitable mate for flowery hues.

Decorative accessories that work well with pastels include gilt-trimmed frames, floral bouquets, green plants, baskets, jewel-toned pillows, botanical prints, wall-hung tapestries, wall-hung plates with floral motifs, and landscapes and seascapes, to name a few. When pastels are used in a beach home or vacation retreat, blue is generally the color of choice, and shell collections, miniature boats, and striped pillows often chime in.

Kitchens and baths are well suited to nature-inspired pastels. In the kitchen, cabinetry can be painted almost any color from soft blue to pale green or yellow to lighten up the space. And in the bath, white fixtures will gleam against your favorite pastel tint. Color coordinate the appropriate accessories, or add complementary colors for added flair. Towels, for instance, are a wonderfully simple means for introducing an accent color into the bath.

Above: A WHITE SPACE TAKES ON RELAXING AND UNDERSTATED BEAUTY WHEN OUTFITTED IN PALE BLUES. THE UPHOLSTERED HEADBOARD, IN A MEDIUM BLUE, BECOMES A STRIKING FOCAL POINT, WHILE THE SOFT BLUE AND WHITE FLORAL SPREAD PROVIDES A GRACEFUL TRANSITION TO THE SURROUNDING WHITENESS. MIXING PATTERNS IS A WONDERFUL WAY OF BLENDING COLORS—AS EVIDENCED BY THE WAY THE BED PRACTICALLY FLOWS INTO THE CHECKERED CHAISE LONGUE.

Right: Pastels mixed with light or bleached woods can run the risk of making a room seem too pale. In this dining room, a soft lavender and white color scheme is indeed blended with light woods, but the pastel hue acts as an accent color (manifesting itself in the chairs and area rug) rather than providing the decorative focus. By introducing a black-and-white photograph and silver objects, the owners have given the space a polished look.

Opposite: Painted pink, the walls in this welcoming living room present a sweet demeanor that's not too syrupy, thanks to the use of white paint on the architectural trim. With pastels, texture becomes an important component of the decor, preventing rooms from appearing too bland. The wicker coffee table and chair, resembling furnishings often found on a porch, bring a taste of the outdoors inside.

Above: While pastels can form the main focus of a color scheme, they can also be used as accents to imbue a room with just a hint of springtime. This casually elegant bedroom, designed with neutral hues that include gray, white, and tan, also features a striking armoire with hand-painted blooms. On the bed, a needlework pillow bearing flowers repeats the subtle infusion of pinks and purples.

Left: TEXTURED GREEN WALLS TEAM UP WITH A FLORAL-PATTERNED CANOPY TO CREATE THE SENSATION OF SLEEPING IN A MEADOW OF WILDFLOWERS. THE PASTEL TINTS OF THE WALLS AND PILLOWS PROVIDE A SOOTHING COUNTERPOINT TO THE STRONGER HUES OF THE FLORAL DESIGN, WHICH IS REPEATED IN THE BEDSIDE ARMCHAIR. THE RESULTING PICTURE IS A PERFECT EXAMPLE OF HOW PASTELS CAN MIX GRACEFULLY WITH OTHER NATURE-INSPIRED HUES.

Above: A BEAUTIFUL PASTEL BLUE, REMINISCENT OF A CLEAR SKY, COVERS THE CEILING AND MUCH OF THE TRIM IN THIS SPACIOUS KITCHEN—AS WELL AS THE LIVING ROOM BEYOND. WHITE CABINETRY, COUNTERTOPS, AND A WHITE TILE BACKSPLASH MAINTAIN THE AIRY QUALITY OF THE SPACE, WHICH HAS BEEN ESTABLISHED BY AN ABUNDANT USE OF GLASS. NOTE THAT DECORATIVE TOUCHES HAVE BEEN KEPT TO A MINIMUM, ALLOWING THE SCENIC COLOR SCHEME TO BE THE FOCUS OF ATTENTION.

Opposite: IN THIS WELCOMING EAT-IN KITCHEN, A WHITE COUNTERTOP AND TILE BACKSPLASH BREAK UP THE EXPANSE OF MINT GREEN WALLS. THE COOL COLOR SCHEME IS WARMED BY A WOODEN HARVEST TABLE AND SIDE TABLE, AS WELL AS SUCH NATURAL ACCENTS AS A BOWL OF ORANGES, A BASKET OF GOURDS, AND A PLANT ARRANGEMENT. BENCHES AT THE TABLE COMBINE WITH THE GREEN BACKGROUND TO CREATE A PICNICLIKE ATMOSPHERE.

Left: APRICOT WALLS ARE A SMART CHOICE FOR A SMALL KITCHEN, SINCE THIS SOFT TINT NOT ONLY MAKES A ROOM APPEAR LARGER, BUT ALSO MAINTAINS THE WARMTH OF A COZY SPACE. HERE, THE APRICOT HUE POPS UP AGAIN IN THE TILE COUNTERTOP, WHILE PALE YELLOW CABINETS PROVIDE A MELODIOUS INTERLUDE. GLEAMING COPPER COOKWARE IS SHOWN OFF TO ADVANTAGE BY THE WALL COLOR, WHILE A LIGHT GREEN VINTAGE STOVE ADDS APPEALING CONTRAST.

Left: PASTELS ARE OFTEN ASSOCIATED WITH COTTAGE DECOR, BUT HERE'S PROOF POSITIVE THAT THEY ARE HIGHLY VERSATILE. IN THIS CONTEMPORARY LIVING ROOM, PALE GREEN WALLS, NEUTRAL CARPETING, AND WHITE SLIPCOVERS ESTABLISH A SERENE TONE THAT HELPS PUT FAMILY MEMBERS AND GUESTS AT EASE. THANKS TO THE SOFT BACKDROP, THE ARTISTIC TABLES, WITH THEIR DEEPER HUES, ARE ALLOWED TO TAKE CENTER STAGE.

Above: WOODEN WAINSCOTING HAS BEEN PAINTED A PASTEL YELLOW TO BRING A TOUCH OF SUNSHINE TO A FORMERLY DARK HALLWAY. THE WHITE BASEBOARD AND UPPER PORTION OF THE WALL HELP TO LIGHTEN THE SPACE FURTHER. THE HORIZONTAL STENCILED BORDER SPORTS YELLOW DIAMONDS THAT LINK IT TO THE WAINSCOT-ING, WHILE THE MOSS-COLORED MOLDING ECHOES THE COLOR OF THE PAINTED TABLE.

Right: HERE, A MONOCHROMATIC PALETTE CALLS UPON VARIOUS TONES OF YELLOW TO CREATE A SUMMERY BATH. DEEP SHADES OF YELLOW IN THE WINDOW DRESSING ARE JOINED BY A PALE YELLOW GRACING THE VANITY AND SHELVES TO FORM A CREAMY BLEND. WHITE PULLS, WHITE FLOWERS, AND A PRIMARILY WHITE MARBLE COUNTER PROVIDE VARIETY AND GIVE THE SPACE A PRIM LOOK.

Calming Blues and Forest Greens

Ask several people what their favorite color is and, undoubtedly, the majority will say blue. It's no wonder—blue promotes a sense of well-being and tranquility. The color of the sky and the sea, it has long been associated with spirituality, royalty, and justice. Its many variations blend splendidly with numerous other colors, and its coolness establishes a peaceful tone when used in the home. While blue is often preferred for bedrooms, thanks to its restful nature, it has also been used for centuries in kitchens throughout Europe, where it is linked to cleanliness and celebrated in the renowned designs of Delft tiles.

Blue and white is a popular combination for both traditional and country decors, but the possibilities don't stop there. Blues can be mixed with greens or yellows, as well as with rich jewel tones, such as gold, burgundy, or crimson, for an elegant look. Highly versatile, blue also provides an attractive, solid splash of color in contemporary settings decked out in grays and other neutral tones. When decorating a room, consider the darker shades, such as navy, sapphire, and cobalt, as well as the mid-range hues, which include sky blue, iris, cornflower blue, turquoise, and French blue. These are but a small sampling of the myriad blues that will evoke the spirit of the outdoors when showcased inside.

Green brings to mind forests and fields, as well as the fruits, vegetables, and flowers that grow within these natural settings. There seems to be no end to the greens found in the countryside, and several of these enchanting hues can be used to create refreshing environments throughout the home. Appropriately, green is symbolic of life and fertility; we have only to look out the window on a spring day and witness the budding green leaves to be reminded of the incredible vitality associated with this color.

Certain greens can be used to create stately backgrounds indoors. For instance, forest green achieves a sedate and refined tone in a library, while a medium green may be just the color to outfit your garden room. Possessing a deeper tone than the pastel tints, such mid-range greens

Opposite: A four-poster bed commands attention in this subdued setting. The walls are painted a sedate green with delicate white veining that hints at tree branches and leaves. A white ceiling and white accents lend an airy quality while maintaining the tranquil tone. Leafy plants are simple touches that complete the picture of a forest glen.

as moss, olive, and sage can be combined with white or cream to form an elegant backdrop. Depending upon the particular shade of green you select, you can add other greens of a similar tone, touches of blue, neutral colors, yellow, pink, or gold.

Both blue and green have played large roles in the history of interior design throughout Europe, so it's no wonder that either color can serve as the starting point for an English country, Scandinavian, Mediterranean, or French country decor. In the annals of North American design, blue has always held a prominent place, while green became fashionable in Victorian and Arts and Crafts decors. Since rigid limits are no longer imposed upon color when it comes to home decorating, blue and/or green can be used with any of the styles mentioned above, as well as for more modern interiors.

As with any color, paint is an excellent means for establishing a blue or green background, but wallpaper may be called upon for texture and panache. Many of the striking Arts and Crafts wallpaper designs made popular by William Morris (and being reproduced today) incorporate beautiful muted shades of blue and green. There are also numerous striped, floral, and geometric patterns to select from, as well as French toile de Jouy wallpapers, which blend quite pleasantly and harmoniously with checked and floral fabrics.

Since deep and medium shades of blue and green have a strength about them, they call for flooring that holds its own. Oak and parquet floors, richly toned wall-to-wall carpeting, and jewel-colored Oriental rugs certainly will not fade into the background, and they work well in living rooms, dining rooms, or bedrooms. Ceramic tile, as well as resilient flooring in one of the many colors and patterns available today, is highly suitable for the kitchen and bath. And speaking of tile, consider the possibilities for designing a decorative backsplash or countertop in the kitchen. Hand-painted tiles will not only provide additional dashes of color, but will also bring an original touch to the setting.

Since medium- or deep-shaded cool colors can establish a peaceful mood, they are often the ideal candidates for a sumptuous window dressing. Rich draperies made of damask, velvet, or a toile de Jouy will imbue a room with semiformal or formal airs, while a crisp gingham or Provençal fabric creates an easygoing feel. Other options include Roman shades, which can be custom-made to match upholstery for a coordinated look, or wooden shutters coated with a dark stain or a white painted finish for a streamlined treatment that has a hint of architectural flair.

Nature-inspired blues and greens can also be introduced into a living room, bedroom, or dining room via furnishings upholstered in these color categories. Stripes, checks, chintz, and other florals can work well, but don't overlook other options, such as a striking paisley or a tartan plaid, both of which can be lovely in a family room or library. Keep in mind, mixing different patterns in a single

room is an effective way of adding visual drama when the color scheme focuses on a single hue. Other furnishings that blend beautifully with blues and greens include darker wood pieces, faux bamboo, metals (with a silver finish), and painted pieces. Picture an indigo blue step-back cupboard in the eat-in kitchen, hunter green bookcases in the study, or Shaker cabinets, wearing their signature gray-blue, in the dining area. In garden rooms, metal and wicker furnishings are often painted green to link the space to the outdoors.

There is a glorious assortment of decorative accessories that can be called upon to give a home distinct touches of blue or green. Rustic pottery, for example, has a certain old-world charm, while glassware sparkles in colors ranging from sea blue to bottle green. Blue and white china is an obvious choice, and a display of willow pattern dishes can be arranged in a glass-front cabinet or situated gallery-style on a prominent wall. Pewter and silver candlesticks make fitting accessories when blues or greens sport a little gray. Even the bath can be dressed to the nines when luxurious towels and fresh flowers are chosen to flatter a blue or green theme. Remember, too, you can change accessories to reflect the seasons, your mood, or the intended purpose of a room.

Above: Timeless elegance is conveyed in a living room where furnishings and windows are dressed in green. White walls and beige carpeting provide a quiet background for a forest green sofa and a toile-covered easy chair with a dark green woodland pattern. This same fabric is used for the window shades to give the room a coordinated look. The checkered wing chair, the mini print on the ottoman, and the floral design on the toss pillow brighten the scene, just like colorful blooms dotting a wilderness setting.

Above: Since green is a mind-soothing color, it's the perfect choice for a home library. Hunter green bookshelves, walls, and mullions give a restful quality to this room devoted to quiet pursuits. In order to temper the darker tones, the owners have incorporated floral curtains, a natural fiber rug, and chunky baskets.

Opposite: BATHED IN BLUE, THIS DINING ROOM CEILING APPEARS TO BRING THE SKY INDOORS. WHITE WALLS ARE ACCENTED WITH THE SAME SHADE OF BLUE ON THE DOOR AND WINDOW FRAMES, ACTING AS A FOIL FOR THE DARK WOOD FURNISHINGS AND HANDSOME WOOD FLOOR. **Right:** SUBTLE INFUSIONS OF BLUE CREATE A PEACEFUL RETREAT IN THIS CHARMING BEDROOM. ON THE CEILING, A PAINTED SKY, COMPLETE WITH SWIRLS OF CLOUDS, CREATES THE FEELING OF SLEEPING OUTDOORS—A SENSATION THAT IS ENHANCED BY THE RUSTIC TWIG FURNISHINGS. INDEED, WITH ITS CANOPIED STYLING, THE BED RESEMBLES A SHELTERING NATURAL BOWER THAT IS SURE TO LULL OCCUPANTS INTO A SOUND SLEEP. ACCENTS OF BLUE, SEEN IN THE BLANKET AND SOFA PILLOWS, ARE SPRINKLED ACROSS THE ROOM TO TIE THE SPACE TOGETHER.

Above: Thanks to a stunning paint treatment, these aquamarine walls resemble a Mediterranean seascape, with wisps of white reminiscent of whitecaps. The cool and serene canvas is warmed by plank flooring, similar to that of a yacht, and a shell-framed mirror that carries out the beach theme. The predominant blue and white color scheme is extended by the bedspread, sheer curtains, velvet upholstery, and architectural details.

Above: IN THIS SPARE BUT ATTRACTIVE BATHROOM, A BEAMED CEILING AND A REDDISH FLOOR ARE COMPLEMENTED BY VARIOUS SHADES OF BLUE, WHICH POP UP ON THE WALLS, TUB SURROUND, CUPBOARD, AND WINDOW FRAME. THE BLUES ENHANCE THE MINIMALIST DECOR WHILE MAINTAINING THE RUSTIC LOOK OF THE SPACE.

Above: Just the right amount of dark green has been introduced into this spacious kitchen—enough to add drama but not overwhelm. The textured wall treatment heightens the natural look, creating a mossy finish. By tempering the walls with a white wood-beamed ceiling, white cabinetry, an earthy tile floor, and wood countertops, the owners have established a reassuring sense of balance. Skylights in the vaulted ceiling provide additional natural lighting so walls don't appear too dark. Note how the color-coordinated lighting fixtures enhance the palette.

—

Right: CUSTOM-CRAFTED CABINETS, WHICH LOOK MORE LIKE ELEGANT FURNISHINGS, DISPLAY A MOSS GREEN TRIM THAT REINFORCES THE GREEN TILE BACKSPLASH AND WINDOW SURROUND. TILE IS AN EFFECTIVE MEANS FOR INTRODUCING BOTH COLOR AND TEXTURE INTO THE KITCHEN. IN THIS PARTICULAR CASE, THE VARIOUS GREEN HUES AT THE WINDOW SEEM TO BRIDGE THE GAP BETWEEN THE INTERIOR AND THE NATURAL BEAUTY BEYOND THE PANES.

Left: ROYAL BLUE WALLS WITH WHITE TRIM GIVE THIS DINING ROOM A MAJESTIC LOOK. WITH THEIR FORMAL AIRS, GILT FRAMES, A STAGGERED DISPLAY OF BLUE AND WHITE CHINA, AND REGAL TASSELS ON THE DINING ROOM CHAIRS CONTRIBUTE TO THE SUMPTUOUS LOOK. VISUAL DRAMA IS INTRODUCED BY THE RED IN THE CUSHIONS, AS WELL AS THE RICH RED PAINT ON THE WALLS OF THE ADJOINING ROOM.

Above: HUNTER GREEN ACCENTS PUNCTUATE A CONTEMPORARY KITCHEN DESIGNED WITH NEUTRAL HUES AND PASTEL GREEN WALLS. BY INTRODUCING A WOODLAND COLOR, THE OWNERS HAVE LINKED THE SPACE TO THE TREES OUTSIDE, SEEN THROUGH THE GLASS-FITTED DOOR. FOR ADDED MEASURE, A FLORAL ARRANGEMENT BOASTING LUSH GREEN LEAVES HAS BEEN PLACED ON THE COUNTER. **Right:** A FRENCH COUNTRY KITCHEN IS COLOR-WASHED WITH DELPHINIUM BLUE. THANKS TO A SOFTENING PAINT TECHNIQUE, THIS STRONG BLUE IS NOT OVERPOWERING. A GENEROUS BANK OF WINDOWS, WHICH AFFORDS PLENTY OF NATURAL LIGHT, ALSO HELPS PREVENT THE SPACE FROM SEEMING TOO INTENSE. GOLDEN WOOD TONES, KITCHEN-WARE ON DISPLAY, AND NATURAL GREENERY GIVE THE ROOM TEXTURE, WHILE A BRIGHT WHITE STOVE, WHICH CAN CLEARLY HOLD ITS OWN AGAINST THE VIVID BACKDROP, CONTRIBUTES CONTRAST.

Left: CORNFLOWER BLUE WALLS HAVE TRANSFORMED THIS BEDROOM INTO A RESTFUL HAVEN. THE COOL BLUE IS ACCENTUATED BY THE USE OF CRISP WHITE ON THE PAINTED FLOOR, MANTEL, CORNICE, AND CEILING. DEEPER BLUES, ALONG WITH HEARTY RED ACCENTS, ARE FEATURED IN THE AREA RUG AND PATCHWORK QUILT, SUPPLYING A GROUNDING SENSE OF DEPTH. A GILT MIRROR AND AN OAK ARMOIRE PITCH IN TO GIVE THE ROOM ADDITIONAL WARMTH.

Opposite: CLASSIC STYLE IS CLEARLY EVIDENT IN THIS SHAKER-INSPIRED BATH. A DEEP GRAY-GREEN PAINT HAS BEEN USED THROUGH-OUT, APPEARING EVEN ON THE SHAKER PEG RACK. COMBINING THIS SEDATE HUE WITH WHITE ACCENTS NOT ONLY ADHERES TO THE LETTER OF SHAKER STYLE, BUT ALSO MAKES THE SPACE MORE INVITING.

Muted Earth Shades and Harvest Colors

There is perhaps nothing more invigorating than a crisp autumn morning. Autumn is the time of year for strolling the aisles of a lively harvest festival, tending the late blooms in the garden, and simply pausing for a moment here and there to take in the colorful view. Goldenrod, burnt umber, ocher, mocha, crimson, russet, pumpkin, terra-cotta, brick, pale gold—these are the colors of changing leaves, late harvests and flowers, pungent spices, and sun-baked earth.

Earth shades and harvest colors are warm hues that bear a subtle tone. Unlike a vibrant red or bright yellow, these colors have an almost aged or muted look that makes them ideal for interior use. Such browns, reds, and yellows can be called upon to fashion cozy country rooms, rustic retreats, or elegant surroundings. Their versatility makes them popular choices for understated and timeless designs on everything from wallpaper and upholstery to bedding and dishware.

Muted earth shades and harvest colors can be mixed with one another or with any number of other colors. White or cream can be used in tandem with these earthy hues to give a room a fresh look. Browns, such as burnt umber and a lighter mocha, can be mixed with brick red, blue, or white, while such yellows as ocher and golden-rod pair up nicely with dark reds or deep blues. In the red category, terra-cotta is set off by adding touches of yellow, blue, or medium green. When paired with gold accents, terra-cotta exudes an especially warm, rich look.

Opposite: RUGGED NATURAL TEXTURE CAN BE A STRONG PURVEYOR OF EARTHY COLOR. HERE, A STONE FIREPLACE PROVIDES A POWERFUL FOCAL POINT WITH ITS MEDLEY OF BROWN HUES. ADDITIONAL BROWNS ARE BROUGHT INTO THE MIX BY THE TONE-ON-TONE SOFA AND UNPAINTED WOODWORK, WHILE TOSS PILLOWS SUPPLY REFRESHING DASHES OF GOLD AND RED. CREAM-COLORED WALLS SERVE AS A WELCOME COUNTERPOINT TO THE HEAVIER HUES OF THE SPACE.

Left: EARTHY COLORS AND A DECORATIVE PAINTING TECHNIQUE RESULT IN AN ENTRYWAY WITH EUROPEAN CHARM. A WARM BURNT SIENNA HAS BEEN CHOSEN FOR THE WALLS, WHILE A LIGHTER RAW SIENNA, FEATURING SOFT BROWN AND PINK TONES, GRACES THE CEILING, MAKING THE SPACE SEEM LARGER. BOTH SURFACES HAVE BEEN SPONGE-PAINTED TO CREATE THE ILLUSION OF TEXTURE; MEANWHILE, AN ORIENTAL RUG AND PLUMP CUSHIONS SUPPLY THE REAL THING.

Earthy hues become all the more beautiful on walls that are color-washed or sponged for a decorative or aged effect. Throughout Italy and France, where such colors predominate, old plaster walls painted in earth shades wear a patina, acquired over time, that reflects the rural countryside. Happily, these same results can be achieved today with patience, time, and minimal skill. How-to books on painting techniques offer step-by-step instructions for achieving the look you desire.

Walls can also be stenciled or dressed with decorative white moldings to set off a palette composed of earth shades. Add a wood-beamed ceiling, and the room is imbued with rustic charm. Of course, if you are fortunate enough to have a brick or stone wall in your home, you can build from this. Wallpapers, too, can be selected in these nature-inspired hues to set a backdrop that works with your particular decorative style.

Possibilities for floors include unglazed terra-cotta tiles, flagstone, pine planking, resilient flooring with a brick pattern, neutral-colored carpeting, and natural fiber rugs. Earthy textures look especially at home with these close-to-the-earth colors and are naturals for a country decor. For a more sophisticated look, carpeting or wood flooring can be layered with Oriental rugs.

Window treatments, depending upon your personal taste and the type of room they will be used in, range from no window dressing at all (to let the view shine) to bamboo shades, matchstick blinds, or heavy drapes.

Shutters, painted white or bearing a light wood stain, can be used to filter light, offer a measure of privacy, and provide substance.

In the living room, dining room, and family room, wood furnishings can be light or dark depending on how casual the room is. Lighter wood tones blended with earth shades and harvest colors are typical of a European country style, while darker woods have a more formal, opulent look and are especially well suited to a traditional decor. Leather sofas and chairs, rush-seat chairs, and bamboo or painted furnishings are a few appropriate options, as are upholstered pieces featuring the colors included in this chapter. Antiques are especially beautiful when showcased against a backdrop of heartening autumnal hues. In bedrooms, you may opt for white furniture and/or bedding to provide contrast against an earthy background.

Kitchens and bathrooms can be stunning when treated to a muted earth shade. Oak cabinetry or cupboards painted white will move your color choice center stage and give the setting a warm, inviting air.

Flattering decorative or finishing touches might include pottery or stoneware, gilt mirrors and picture frames, throw pillows with tassels or fringe, warm throws in neutral hues or earth shades, leather-bound books, baskets for their natural texture, flowers and plants, and brass candlesticks. Don't underestimate the power of accessories, which should be chosen to complement the look and tone of the space.

Right: THIS CONTEMPORARY LIVING ROOM USES A VARIETY OF HARVEST COLORS TO PROVIDE A WARM BACKDROP FOR FURNISHINGS DECKED OUT IN PALE NEUTRAL HUES. A PAIR OF GARNET RED PILLOWS IS ALL IT TAKES TO LINK THE SOFA WITH THE LARGE PIECE OF ART IN THE BACKGROUND. SO THAT THE CONTRAST BETWEEN THE DEEP RED AND LIGHT BEIGE ON THE SOFA IS NOT TOO STARK, A MUTED BLUE-GRAY PILLOW FILLS IN THE GAP AND EASES THE TRANSITION.

Left: THE RICH BROWNS IN THIS SUMPTUOUS LIVING ROOM ARE REMINISCENT OF EXOTIC SPICES OR AUTUMN LEAVES. OCHER WALLS AND CREAMY CARPETING SET THE STAGE FOR THE ARRAY OF BROWN TONES PRESENTED BY THE MOCHA DRAPES AND WINDOW SHADE, THE UPHOLSTERED CHAIRS, AND THE FAWN-COLORED SOFA. LUXURIOUS FABRICS, SUCH AS VELVET OR SATIN, WORK ESPECIALLY WELL WITH A STRONG COLOR, AS THEY TEND TO BRING OUT THE HUE'S LUSTER.

Below: A LUMINOUS GOLDEN BACKDROP DRESSES UP THIS COUNTRY INTERIOR WITH A SLIGHTLY FORMAL AIR, WHICH IS ENHANCED BY THE RICH RED AND GOLD VALANCE. THE PAINTING TECHNIQUE USED TO AGE THE WALLS GIVES THE ROOM A SENSE OF HISTORY.

Opposite: DRAMATIC IMPACT IS THE RESULT WHEN WALLS ARE PAINTED A SATURATED MARIGOLD HUE. BACKING UP A DEEP GREEN FIREPLACE, THE INTENSE COLOR JAZZES UP THE SETTING AND ENERGIZES THE SPACE.

Above: SALMON-COLORED WALLS IMBUE THIS LIVING ROOM WITH ELEGANCE. THE COLOR BLENDS EFFORTLESSLY WITH THE WARM REDS, GOLDS, AND BROWNS, WHICH POP UP IN THE TABLE SKIRT, LAMP, AND TOSS PILLOWS. VELVETY MOSS GREEN UPHOLSTERY ENTICES VISITORS TO MAKE THEMSELVES COMFORTABLE ON THE SETTEE AND PROVIDES GROUNDING CONTRAST. AGAINST THE ORANGISH TONES OF THE BACKDROP, GILT FRAMES ACQUIRE A RICH LOOK.

Opposite: WITH THE HELP OF SOFT LIGHTING, RICH BROWN WALLS BEARING HINTS OF ORANGE CAST A BEAUTIFUL GLOW, IMBUING THIS DINING ROOM WITH A FEELING OF INTIMACY. COLOR CONTINUITY IS ACHIEVED IN THE DINING AREA AND ADJOINING LIVING ROOM WITH THE HELP OF RUGS THAT FEATURE STRONG BLUES. **Right:** A PALE SHADE OF TERRA-COTTA ADDS GENTLE COLOR TO THIS STATELY SETTING. RECALLING THE SIMPLE BEAUTY OF SUN-BAKED CLAY POTS, THIS HUE IS EASY TO LIVE WITH AND MADE ALL THE MORE BEAUTIFUL WHEN BLENDED WITH DARK WOOD TONES. NOTICE HOW THE USE OF OPEN SHELVING ALLOWS THE EARTHY HUE TO SHINE THROUGH, HEIGHTENING THE APPEAL OF THE CHINA DISPLAY. THE BLUE AND WHITE COMBINATION IS REPEATED IN THE AREA RUG, OFFERING SUBTLE CONTRAST AT DIFFERENT LEVELS.

Above: CALLING UPON THE COLORS OF AUTUMN LEAVES, THIS SPACIOUS BEDROOM PRESENTS A BREATHTAKING BLEND OF REDS, ORANGES, YELLOWS, AND BROWNS.

THE USE OF SIMILAR TONES HEIGHTENS THE HARMONY OF THE SCENE, AND THE WARMTH OF THE COLORS MAKES THE LARGE ROOM SEEM COZY.

Right: DRAMATIC WHEN USED ON A LARGE SCALE, BROWN TENDS TO HAVE MASCULINE OVERTONES. THIS QUALITY IS TEMPERED HERE BY SOFT TOUCHES, SUCH AS THE PURPLE AND WINE-COLORED CANOPY ABOVE THE BED AND THE PATTERNED THROW.

Opposite: COLOR CONTINUITY IS AN EFFECTIVE STRATEGY WHEN ROOMS ARE ON DISPLAY FROM OTHER AREAS OF THE HOME. HERE, THE DINING ROOM AND KITCHEN ARE CONNECTED BY THE COMPATIBLE HUES OF THEIR WALLS— SCARLET IN THE FORMER, AND A GOLDEN BROWN IN THE LATTER. NOTICE HOW THE SPONGING TECHNIQUE USED ON THE KITCHEN WALLS CREATES A SUBTLE MIX OF TONES, RESULTING IN A TEXTURED APPEARANCE. ARCHITECTURAL FEATURES IN BOTH ROOMS ARE HIGHLIGHTED IN WHITE. **Right:** MUTED TERRA-COTTA TILES FORM A NATURAL-LOOKING BACKSPLASH AND COUNTERTOP IN THIS PROVINCIAL KITCHEN. A BRASS FAUCET MAINTAINS THE WARM LOOK, WHILE THE PATTERNED WALLPAPER TRIM ON THE WINDOW LEDGE LIGHTENS UP THE SCENE A LITTLE WITH ITS SUBDUED PALE GOLDEN HUE. FOR LOVELY COLOR CONTRAST, BLUE CERAMIC POTS PLANTED WITH FLOWERS LINE UP ON THE SILL.

Left: TILE IS A DECORATOR'S DREAM WHEN IT COMES TO GIVING A KITCHEN A DOSE OF COLOR AND PERSONALITY. HERE, THE BACKSPLASH IS PRIMARILY COMPOSED OF EARTH-COLORED TILES, LIGHT AND DARK, WHICH LINK IT TO THE SURROUNDING WOODEN ELEMENTS. SAPPHIRE BLUE TILES POP UP THROUGHOUT THE MIX TO PROVIDE CONTRAST AND TO HELP DRAW THE EYE. UNDER-THE-CABINET FIXTURES NOT ONLY OFFER GREAT TASK LIGHTING, BUT ALSO PLAY UP THE VARIATIONS IN COLOR.

Left: CREAMY FLOORING, WHITE TRIM, A WHITE PEDESTAL SINK, AND A WHITE WINDOW DRESSING PLAY UP WARM OCHER WALLS. A BLACK METAL TOWEL STAND AND A CLASSIC CHAIR WITH BLUE UPHOLSTERY ADD COLOR CONTRAST. ELEGANT TOUCHES, INCLUDING TASSELS AND A GILT MIRROR, IMBUE THE BATH WITH TIMELESS STYLE.

Left: A HARMONIOUS INTERPLAY OF DIFFERENT BROWNS, TEXTURES, AND MATERIALS CONTRIBUTES TO THE RICHNESS OF THIS BATHROOM. NOTICE HOW THE GRAINING OF THE WOOD AND THE SWIRLS AND FLECKS OF THE MARBLE PROVIDE NATURAL DECORATION.

PART THREE
BLUE & WHITE ROOMS

INTRODUCTION

When I was five, I thought the prettiest shades of blue were in the tiny forget-me-nots and climbing morning glories of my parents' garden. Nearly twenty summers later, while honeymooning in Bermuda, I was romanced by the more dazzling blue of the aquamarine Atlantic Ocean. And then, one beautiful autumn in Illinois, my husband and I discovered the most precious blue of all—the luminous ultramarine of our newborn daughter's eyes.

Chances are good that a variety of blues will remind you of beautiful things, breathtaking landscapes, and the people you love. Around the world, blue magically captivates, for it is a regal hue with a rich history. Just as revered, however, is the combination of blue and white, a contrasting duet of colors that is always exciting and refreshing. For centuries, alluring shades of indigo, cobalt, turquoise, and robin's-egg blue have dovetailed with white in priceless Chinese porcelains, exotic Moroccan tiles, lovely Dutch delft china, French toile de Jouy fabric, cozy American quilts, and lyrical paintings by celebrated artists.

The color blue has been highly regarded through the ages, not only for its beauty, but because for many centuries it was a rare luxury. To create an ultramarine paint for royal palaces, temples, and tombs, the ancient Egyptians would grind precious lapis lazuli stones into fine powder, or dissolve compounded copper salts with resin. Later, the ancient Greeks produced a wider range of blues by experimenting with copper, iron, and mercury. It wasn't until the twelfth century A.D. that ultramarine was introduced to Europe, and even then, it was so expensive that it was only used by painters. By the eighteenth century, however, the British East India Company imported affordable indigo dyes to Europe, and Prussian blue, the first synthetic blue pigment, was produced. During the Victorian era, new synthetic dyes added blue-greens and purples to the rainbow of textile and paint colors.

Historically, many civilizations have considered blue and white to be enriching or virtuous colors. To early Egyptians, blue represented celestial light and justice. In

Opposite: DETAILS SUCH AS THE FEDERAL SHIELD-BACK ARMCHAIR, THE STRIPED BLUE AND WHITE WALLPAPER, AND THE LOVELY BALLOON SHADES ADD A SENSE OF YESTERDAY TO THIS ELEGANTLY APPOINTED LIVING ROOM.

ancient Greece, blue stood for altruism and integrity, while white denoted purity. During the Middle Ages, the Church believed that white symbolized purity and blue represented spiritual love or truth.

Today, blue is a color that signifies tranquillity, spirituality, trustworthiness, and infinity. Bold, vivid blues are also associated with high drama and energy. White is a valuable neutral color that comes in numerous shades, from bright titanium to gentle magnolia, vanilla, ivory, and cream. White can contrast smartly with royal or navy blues. It can also soften blue's bold personality and create a visual resting point in a room.

Whatever blissful blue and white interiors you envision, it's helpful to remember that blue's refreshing coolness is greatly affected by surrounding hues. It's important to pay attention to color temperature when decorating: blue, green, and violet are the cool colors of the spectrum, while red, orange, and yellow are warm hues that radiate more light and heat. By following a few simple guidelines you can warm your blue and white palette and avoid unintentionally creating a melancholy room.

Be sure to consider your room's lighting. If its windows face north, the room will likely receive limited, bluish-toned light that needs to be perked up with accents in warm colors such as yellow or scarlet. On the other hand, a southern exposure will probably be sunny and appropriate for dazzling, pure blue and white schemes. Also, keep in mind that incandescent light bulbs can add a warm, yellow glow, while fluorescent fixtures will cool the atmosphere with pale blue light, and halogen lamps may sap the richness from your colors.

Before you pick up a paintbrush or look for a new wallpaper pattern, it's a good idea to immerse yourself in a sea of blue and white possibilities. The following pages will take you across the globe and back through time to explore eight decorating styles that offer captivating interpretations of the blue and white theme: traditional Federal, Regency, and Victorian styles; distinctive country styles from North America, Scandinavia, France, and the Mediterranean; and the clean contemporary style.

America's Federal style, which was popular in the late eighteenth and early nineteenth centuries, was a celebration of America's status as a powerful, expanding young republic. The Federal style was inspired by the neoclassical decors and furnishings of the French Empire and English Regency styles, but often incorporated such patriotic symbols as the eagle instead of traditional classic motifs.

The elegant, airy English Regency style came into vogue when George IV became Prince Regent in 1811. Regency style took inspiration from the architecture and colors of ancient Greece and Rome, as well as the regal French Empire style popularized during Napoleon's reign. Vibrant contrasting colors were paired together, which complemented furnishings and architectural moldings that incorporated such ancient motifs as honeysuckles, lyres, shells, and Greek keys.

Above, left: WHILE WHITE AND PASTEL BLUES VISUALLY ENLARGE A LIVING SPACE, DARKER BLUES ADVANCE, MAKING A ROOM APPEAR MORE INTIMATE. THIS CONTEMPORARY KITCHEN ACHIEVES A SENSE OF COZINESS WITH ITS DEEP THISTLE-BLUE CABINETS, WHICH CONTRAST BEAUTIFULLY WITH WHITE CUPBOARDS AND TILES AND A PALE WOODEN COUNTER. **Above, right:** ROYAL BLUE PAINT HAS BEEN SPONGED ON THE WALLS OF THIS COMBINED LIBRARY AND DINING ROOM, GIVING A CONTEMPORARY TWIST TO THE TRADITIONAL NEOCLASSICAL DECOR. THE BRIGHT WHITE FIREPLACE IS EMBELLISHED WITH IONIC "COLUMNS."

Interiors of the Victorian period were often done in dark, rich, earthy colors—a sharp contrast to the bright hues of the Regency era. Formal rooms were dressed in a plethora of patterns, colors, and ornaments. Flora and fauna wallpapers were favored, as were plush fabrics with tassels, overstuffed upholstery, knickknacks, and heavy, dark wooden furnishings.

Blue and white have been the colors of choice for numerous country decorating schemes, warming up eclectic gatherings of faded furnishings and the rustic textures of wood, brick, and stone. American country style is known for its array of simple wooden furnishings and muted milk-paint hues. Blue and white are popular colors for such key accessories as patchwork quilts, braided rugs, and graniteware.

Scandinavian country style is easily recognized by its furniture painted with floral designs (called rosemaling), its use of bright colors as accents, and its preference for light-colored woods. Scandinavian style was popularized around 1900 by Swedish artist Carl Larsson. He detested dark, cluttered Victorian decors and wanted to introduce a pleasant, orderly mix of simple furnishings and pale hues that would reflect maximum light—sunshine is a precious commodity in Scandinavian countries.

Both French and Mediterranean country styles are awash in vivid hues appropriate to a sun-drenched climate. French country originated in Provence, which is known for its fragrant flowers and herbs as well as its lively cotton prints and charming style of decor. The wide Mediterranean Sea has inspired another style of vibrant country decor. The clean, spare looks of this style, with its thick, white walls of stone or plaster and weathered blue doors and shutters, can be seen throughout southern Europe and northern Africa.

In a contemporary setting, blue and white create a crisp ambience that is invigorating and fresh. Clean lines and minimal furnishings and accessories often characterize contemporary decors, which celebrate light, texture, color, and form, taking inspiration from any number of simple, elegant decorating styles. A myriad of vivid blue and white appliances, furnishings, wall and floor treatments, and fabrics featuring geometric prints and sprawling patterns have indeed created a look that's both atmospheric and inviting.

OPPOSITE: THIS AMERICAN COUNTRY BEDROOM EVOKES SEASIDE COTTAGE MEMORIES WITH ITS IRIS BLUE, INDIGO, AND WHITE FABRICS AND ACCESSORIES. THE WHALE MOTIF IN THE FRAMED PRINTS IS REPEATED IN THE CURTAINS.

Tranquil Outdoor Living Spaces and Enchanted Gardens

White, ivory, gray-blue, and teal are colors that blend effortlessly with earth and sky, so it's not surprising that more and more homeowners are choosing these soft, natural hues. Porches and other outdoor living spaces are in vogue again, as are tranquil garden "rooms" in summery blues and whites.

White has long been a favorite color choice for the façades of contemporary and country homes, as well as traditional Colonial, Greek Revival, and Victorian houses. These typically feature contrasting blue, black, or green shutters and matching front doors. The façades of more ornate Victorian homes, however, may feature up to five different hues, sometimes incorporating a palette of pale and medium blues and whites.

White is also a popular choice for any number of country- and contemporary-style homes around the world. Countless French and Mediterranean country homes reflect the dazzling sun with thick, whitewashed or tinted stucco walls accented with brightly painted azure shutters and doors and warm terra-cotta tiled roofs and courtyards. In Scandinavia, country home interiors may feature resplendent pale blue walls, but the timber exteriors are often painted red, yellow, or green, accentuated by white shutters and gingerbread trim.

No matter what shade your home's façade wears, it can serve as a lovely backdrop for such outdoor living spaces as porches, patios, decks, courtyards, terraces, gazebos, and loggias, which are columned, open-air spaces on the side of a home. Also, if you live in a temperate climate, you can create a lush "outdoor" room inside your home with a glass-enclosed conservatory or sunroom. The conservatory was especially beloved

Opposite: This Mediterranean-inspired outdoor space is a symphony in blue with custom-designed blue and white tile murals and a dazzling pool.

during the Victorian era and is enjoying renewed popularity today in Europe and North America. The sunroom has also become a popular "greenhouse" space where flowers and families can soak up winter sunshine together. Blue and white are the ideal hues for any of these sanctuaries and can be introduced through a variety of paints, tiles, floorings, furnishings, and accessories.

Wooden porches, loggias, and gazebos can be painted or stained white, cream, blue, or silvery gray, while their ceilings can be painted a pale blue and airbrushed with wisps of white clouds to suggest the ethereal heavens. This decorating tradition was popular during the Victorian era and was inspired by the lifelike painted ceilings favored during the Renaissance.

If your home is graced with an open-air courtyard, terrace, or patio, you can take a cue from brilliant Mediterranean country homes and surround outdoor fountains, pools, rose gardens, or dining areas with tinted cement walkways inset with blue and white stones or blue and white geometric tiles from Morocco or Mexico. Rustic gray-blue unglazed quarry tiles or blue slate dimension stones are other striking ways to add blue to your home's outdoor living areas.

There is an endless variety of outdoor furniture available today, which enables you to interpret your personal style and colors in a contemporary, traditional, or country fashion. Contemporary furnishing styles include sleek steel-framed motel chairs in aqua or pale blue as well as synthetic wicker chairs in white or cobalt. Country and traditional homes can be graced with lovely garden benches, rockers, chairs, and tables made from teak, redwood, pressure-treated pine, or kiln-dried oak as well as with white or teal-blue cast-iron settees, chairs, and tables. Elegant cast- or wrought-aluminum designs can add international flavor to your outdoor rooms, mirroring the romantic furnishings of Arabian courtyards and Parisian cafés. You can also revive wooden furniture with fresh coats of Mediterranean blue, turquoise, or indigo paint.

Beyond the porch or within the courtyard walls, blue and white gardens are perfect places for heart-to-heart talks and leisurely breakfasts accompanied by birdsong. It's been said that a blue garden is good for the body and soul, since gazing at a sea of blue flowers can reduce your body temperature, slow your pulse rate, and quiet your appetite. By introducing white flowers into your garden, you add visual contrast, yet you maintain the graceful aura that only blue can radiate.

When designing a garden "room" in your favorite colors, you can literally take your love for blue and white to new heights. Tall trellises, pergolas, and arbors can simulate walls for morning glories, roses, and clematis to climb, while stone or tile pathways can suggest rustic floors under the sky's eternal blue ceiling. Garden furnishings provide a place to relax and enjoy the beauty of the outdoors, while sculpted ornaments of Buddhas, sprites, or mythological animals lend gracious personality. The most exciting aspect of designing a blue and white garden sanctuary is, of course, selecting an assortment of beautiful blue and white flowers to create your own tapestry of color, texture, and shape.

There's a wide variety of delicate and hardy blooms in this palette from which to choose, and it's wise to read a few gardening books and magazines to find out which flowers will thrive best in your climate. Classic blue posies for beds and borders include forget-me-nots, pansies, blue flax, lobelia, Veronica, and blue phlox. These stand out when they are surrounded by snowy lily of the valley, baby's breath, sweet William, and white violets. For cottage gardens, a mixture of exuberant white and violet irises, blue hydrangea, delphinium, larkspur, blue salvia, Canterbury bells, and the turquoise-hued Himalayan blue poppy can contrast elegantly with white roses, lupines, shasta daisies, and hollyhocks. As Henry David Thoreau said, "Heaven is under our feet, as well as over our heads." This was never more beautifully illustrated than in the enchanted blue and white garden.

Above: BLUE CORNFLOWERS AND PURE WHITE HYDRANGEAS COMPLEMENT THE SKY BLUE OF THIS SIMPLE PLANK TABLE AND ITS MATCHING BENCH. THE TERRA-COTTA VASE AND THE BRICK FLOOR PROVIDE A WARM CONTRAST TO THE COOL BLUES AND GREENS OF THIS GARDEN SPACE.

Opposite: PURE RED AND YELLOW ARE WARM HUES, WHILE BLUE IS REFRESHINGLY COOL. YET SOME BLUES SEEM WARMER BECAUSE THEY CONTAIN A TOUCH OF YELLOW, SUCH AS THE STRIKING BLUE-GREEN OF THIS SUNROOM'S ARMOIRE AND TILED FLOOR. **Above:** FROM THE PATTERNED TABLECLOTHS TO THE FINE CRYSTAL, CURVACEOUS WHITE CHAIRS, AND TINY LAMPSHADES, THIS ALFRESCO SETTING BLENDS SEAMLESSLY WITH NATURE, ECHOING THE GRACEFUL BLUES OF SEA AND SKY.

Opposite: THIS MEDITERRANEAN HOME'S ROMANTIC COURTYARD IS HIGHLIGHTED BY A CONTEMPORARY FOUNTAIN FASHIONED FROM AZURE BLUE TILES. THE TERRA-COTTA POTS OF FLOWERS ADD WARMTH TO THIS MAGICAL SETTING. AZURE WAS A POPULAR WALL COLOR IN POMPEII AND HERCULANEUM, THE ANCIENT ITALIAN CITIES WHOSE TREASURES, EXCAVATED IN THE 1770S, INSPIRED THE VIVID PALETTES AND NEOCLASSICAL DESIGNS FOUND IN REGENCY, FEDERAL, AND EMPIRE DECORS. **Above, left:** IN SUN-DRENCHED REGIONS WHERE HOMES ARE OFTEN PAINTED A BRILLIANT WHITE OR COOL SHERBET HUE, IT'S COMMON TO COLOR DOORWAYS IN A DEEP, VIBRANT BLUE. IN THE MIDDLE EAST AND IN SOME NATIVE AMERICAN COMMUNITIES, DOORWAYS HAVE HISTORICALLY BEEN PAINTED BLUE TO WARD OFF EVIL SPIRITS. **Above, right:** BECAUSE BRIGHT SUNSHINE CAN OVERWHELM PASTEL HUES, THIS MEDITERRANEAN-INSPIRED LOGGIA IS DONE IN EARTH TONES, HIGHLIGHTED BY A DAZZLING BLUE DOORWAY AND A SIMPLE, CONTEMPORARY CHAIR.

Left: A WASH OF APOTHECARY BLUE ENLIVENS THIS TALL COUNTRY FENCE, WHILE SPOTLIGHTING A DAZZLING GARDEN OF SNOWY WHITE FLOWERS. **Opposite:** THE DETAILS OF THIS HOME'S FAÇADE PAINT A PICTURE OF TRADITIONAL REFINEMENT. THE FANLIGHT OVER THE FRONT DOOR, THE VICTORIAN-STYLE IRON FENCE, AND THE BLUE AND WHITE COLOR SCHEME REFLECT AN APPRECIATION FOR CLASSIC ARCHITECTURAL DETAILS AND COLORS.

Opposite: BLUE-VIOLET AND SNOW-WHITE DELPHINIUM ARE THE STARS OF THIS LUSH, VERDANT GARDEN.

Above: IN THIS EXQUISITE GARDEN "ROOM," VISITORS FEEL A SENSE OF SERENITY, FOR LOOKING AT AN EXPANSE OF BLUE FLOWERS

CAN SLOW THE PULSE RATE AS WELL AS DELIGHT THE SOUL. NOTE HOW THE WHITE FLOWERS AND THE PORCELAIN PLANTERS

PROVIDE CONTRAST TO THE PALE AND DEEP BLUE BLOOMS.

Welcoming Rooms Serenaded in Blue

As the gateway to your home, your entryway is a place for daily comings and goings as well as emotional reunions and farewells. Down the hall, your living room or family room serves as a mecca for socializing and relaxing. Whatever your decorating style, a blue and white scheme can bring timeless beauty and color magic to each of these welcoming rooms.

Regency and Federal decors favor the bright French Empire style, so they share similar wall coverings, paint colors, furnishings, and window treatments. Regency and Federal entryways often feature flagstone, varnished wood, or mosaic floors and delicately proportioned neoclassical furnishings. Typical furnishings and accessories include shield-back chairs, gilded tables and mirrors, and chandeliers and torchères.

Regency and Federal drawing rooms can carry out a blue and white theme through resplendent white fireplaces covered with delftware tiles or neoclassical carvings; gracious solid or striped damask upholstery on Grecian couches; blue Aubusson carpets; and layered window treatments that include muslin undercurtains, Wedgwood blue or deep blue silk curtains, and Gothic scalloped valances with tassels. Traditional wallpapers include imitation marble, blue and white Regency stripes, sprigged florals, and blue and gray scenic wallpapers from China or France. Favored paint colors include Federal apothecary blue or cream and such Regency medium blues as sapphire, cerulean, or cobalt. Porcelain vases and urns by Wedgwood, Minton, or Spode reinforce the tranquil color scheme.

High-style Victorian entry halls and parlors often employ dark and light palettes of blue and white. An entryway done in a traditional deep blue embossed wallpaper is the ideal background for gilded mirrors and framed prints, an ornate mahogany table graced with a Tiffany lamp, a blue velvet chair, and an Oriental carpet in

Opposite: In this inviting Regency-style living room, blue and cream toile de Jouy wallpaper and fabric harmonize with neutral carpeting and complementary pillows. Gentle lighting and deep pink flowers add warmth.

sapphire and gold. In the living room, the ceiling might be painted white or pale blue, while the walls could be covered in a blue and white striped wallpaper, accented by light blue molding. Windows can have lace undercurtains topped by pale blue or rose chintz curtains and a blue fringed valance. Other blue touches could include an Oriental carpet, gilded Rococo Revival chairs, a settee upholstered in a pale blue damask, and a mahogany whatnot filled with Chinese porcelain and delftware.

Country-style entryways are less formal than those in traditional homes, yet they exude a gracious ambience. Country entry hall floors can be done in terra-cotta or dimension stone tiles, natural wood, or wood that's been painted or stenciled. Walls may be whitewashed or painted in pastel or medium blues. Decorative wall accents include stenciling, wallpaper borders, blue or white wainscoting, and a painted dado rail. Simple furnishings are best, such as old wooden benches, cast-iron chairs with blue and white gingham cushions, and antique coatracks.

A bright mood can be created in American country living rooms and family rooms with cream-colored walls highlighted by blue trim, stenciling, or wallpaper borders. Wooden floors may be topped with blue braided or hooked rugs, and windows graced with simple white shutters. Key color accents include a Prussian blue camelback sofa topped by an indigo and white quilt, Windsor chairs with calico cushions, and cobalt-glazed crocks filled with wildflowers.

The hallmark pastel blue walls of many Scandinavian country living rooms invite precious light to radiate throughout the home. These walls are often embellished with tongue-and-groove cladding or painted floral borders. Bleached wooden floors are accented with striped runners, while windows wear wispy muslin or lace swags. Traditional Scandinavian country furnishings are a joyful mix of contemporary blonde or painted wood pieces and treasured heirlooms. Common patterns for sofas and pillows include blue and white stripes and ever-popular ginghams. Key accessories include delftware, brass or wrought-iron candlesticks with thin white candles, and pots of summery red geraniums.

In French country homes, strong colors and earthy textures are everywhere. Thick stone or clay living room walls are often left radiantly white, but they can be tinted lavender or sky blue. Ceilings often reveal exposed beams, and floors radiate warmth through dark wood planks or terra-cotta tiles topped with cobalt blue floral rugs. Windows are barely dressed in lacy café curtains, swags, or wooden shutters. Comfort is offered by an assortment of curvaceous walnut or fruitwood furnishings and cozy upholstered chairs. A traditional wooden armoire, hand-painted or carved with botanical motifs, is typically the focal point of the room. Another key French country furnishing is the rush-seated banquette, a bench that can be topped with pillows in azure blue and white checks, paisleys, and traditional Provençal cottons.

In Mediterranean country living rooms, thick stone walls and ceilings are whitewashed, while trim is painted a brilliant blue to provide contrast. Brick, flagstone, or tile flooring is appropriate, as are sisal mats and brightly hued rugs. Sofas and chairs are often made of heavy, ebony-hued wood and sit close to the floor, where the air is refreshingly cool. Other common furnishings include rustic chests and tall cupboards for storage. Colorful accessories include cobalt blue and white pots filled with plants and flowers, turquoise and white wall hangings, and sky blue and white striped or checked pillows.

Like country settings, contemporary decors celebrate simplicity and vibrant hues. A minimalist blue and white entry hall might feature white brick walls and a pale azure ceiling with blonde parquet or white marble flooring. Contemporary furnishings include gleaming metal chairs, torchère-style lamps, and a glass-topped table displaying a clear or blue glass bowl filled with irises. In the living room, an ultramarine ceiling might be softened by white walls, or one gallerylike royal blue wall could be surrounded by vanilla walls and ceiling. Modular furniture in solid cobalt or cream can be grounded by a textured sisal rug. Other important touches include primary-color paintings, sleek marble tables, white lamps, blue glass candlesticks, white vertical blinds, and accent pillows in red, green, apricot, and yellow.

Above: A shrine to nature's beauty, this American country living room's windows rise up to capture the sunlight, while the exposed beams reflect the rich patina of weathered wood and the fireplace offers the texture of old stones. Beautiful blue and white furniture and Chinese porcelain recall the many hues of the sky, while the tall armoire and red Oriental carpet radiate warmth.

Left: THE SCANDINAVIAN LOVE OF SIMPLE YET FUNCTIONAL FURNISHINGS IS REFLECTED IN THIS BACK-DOOR HALLWAY, WHERE THE BLEACHED WOODEN FLOOR HAS BEEN STAINED WITH AN ULTRA-MARINE ANILINE DYE AND SEALED WITH MARINE VARNISH.

Right: GLOWING WITH THE
GOLDEN SUNLIGHT OF LATE AFTER-
NOON, THIS FRONT ROOM'S
POWDER BLUE AND IVORY COLOR
SCHEME SEEMS POSITIVELY WARM.
THE DELICATE SHELL STENCIL ON THE
CHAIR TAKES ITS INSPIRATION FROM
THE NEARBY OCEAN.

Above, left: THE CURVACEOUS FRUITWOOD CHAIRS AND TABLE, INTOXICATING FRESH FLOWERS, CHINESE PORCELAINS, AND INDIGO WALLS SUGGEST A FRENCH COUNTRY MOOD IN THIS DELIGHTFUL FOYER. **Above, right:** GRACEFUL STATUARY AND NEOCLASSICAL MOTIFS ADORN THIS FORMAL PALE TURQUOISE AND WHITE LIVING ROOM. **Opposite:** THIS FAMILY ROOM IS ENERGIZED BY SAND AND SURF HUES AND AN ECLECTIC DECOR THAT BLENDS CONTEMPORARY FABRICS, MEDITERRANEAN FLOOR TILES, THE SUNFLOWERS SO BELOVED IN FRANCE, AND ART INSPIRED BY NATIVE AMERICAN CULTURES.

Opposite: IN THIS ELEGANT MEXICAN HOME, BLUE AND WHITE FURNISHINGS AND DETAILS PROVIDE A REGAL AMBIENCE APPROPRIATE FOR THE DISPLAY OF TREASURED FAMILY HEIRLOOMS. **Right:** FOR CENTURIES, BLUE AND WHITE HAVE ADDED BEAUTY TO FABRICS, FURNITURE, WALLPAPERS, FLOOR TREATMENTS, AND MYRIAD ACCESSORIES. HERE, AN ECLECTIC AMERICAN LIVING ROOM CELEBRATES THE PATRIOTIC FIRE OF RED, WHITE, AND BLUE AGAINST A BACKGROUND OF VIBRANT SAPPHIRE. **Below:** THE BLACK AND WHITE FIREPLACE OF THIS TRADITIONAL LIVING ROOM PRESENTS AN APPEALING CONTRAST OF DARK AND LIGHT COLORS. SO, TOO, DO THE VIVID CHECKS OF THE COZY CHAIR AND CURTAINS, FOR BLUE AND WHITE MAKE AN UNDENIABLY STRONG COLOR COMBINATION.

Above: INSPIRED BY THE LOVELY BLUE AND WHITE PORCELAIN THAT CHINA IS FAMOUS FOR, THE PICTORIAL FABRIC USED FOR THE CHAISE, THROW PILLOWS, AND CURTAIN TRIM BRINGS VITALITY AND CHARM TO THIS PRISTINE WHITE LIVING ROOM.

Opposite: ANCHORED BY A SOLID COBALT BLUE SOFA AND SKY BLUE WALLS, THIS AMERICAN COUNTRY LIVING ROOM MIXES STRIPES, CHECKS, AND FLORALS IN A SPIRITED BLUE, WHITE, AND YELLOW DECOR.

Blue Sky Kitchens and Dining Rooms

As the heart of the home, the kitchen is often a multipurpose room for preparing and eating meals, socializing, watching television, and engaging in hobbies. And, despite our busy lifestyles, the dining room is still a treasured place in our homes, for it reminds us to take time to enjoy the pleasures of entertaining friends and family.

Kitchens can be enlivened by using blue and white on almost every surface. A wide variety of scrubbable wallpapers and semigloss paints are ideal for this highly trafficked room. Some popular flooring choices include vinyl sheet or tiles; ceramic, stone, and terra-cotta tiles; and richly speckled terrazzo made of marble, colored glass, and stone. Blue and white can also capture attention when used in the sink backsplash, countertops, appliances, textiles, and small accessories.

The walls and floor are ideal places to include color in the dining room. Solid blue or blue and white patterned wallpaper can add subtle or flamboyant flair, providing a textured background for paintings, lighting fixtures, and sideboard displays of colorful china and glassware. As the "fifth wall" of your dining room, the floor can be covered with a luxurious azure Oriental or Aubusson carpet, a blue braided rug, or a neutral sisal rug.

Regency- or Federal-inspired kitchens are often painted apothecary blue or cream, or are papered with such patterns as eagles, laurel wreaths, or the Napoleon bee, while the walls in the dining room generally have the same treatment as those in the living room. Federal kitchens might have a blue-hued pine hutch and a gate-leg table with Windsor chairs, while Regency-style kitchens can be graced with a collection of porcelain in a gilded cupboard and floral prints hung with ribbons. In the dining room, both design styles commonly showcase a marble fireplace with Greek motifs and a mantel displaying Chinese ginger jars. Sumptuous furnishings include a neoclassical satinwood table and chairs, a matching sideboard and china cabinet, and such accessories as torchères, a gilded mirror, and ancestral paintings.

Victorians preferred an entirely white kitchen, but modern interpretations of the style often include one other

Opposite: Blue, white, and yellow make up a surefire color scheme for an energetic kitchen. This breakfast nook gleefully mixes contemporary lighting with American country chairs and flooring, primitive carved birds, and a variety of new and old dinnerware.

color. Classic Victorian kitchens have white, mahogany, or oak cupboards with glass fronts and porcelain knobs, as well as oak pedestal tables and chairs, lace curtains, blue and white ceramic or parquet floor tiles, and hanging lamps with colored or frosted glass globes. Kitchen walls can have pale blue or cream semigloss paint or a blue floral wallpaper above white wainscoting, while a dining room looks splendid in a deep blue Rococo, chintz, or Arts and Crafts wallpaper. The typical dining table is mahogany clothed with lace or linen and set with fine silver, crystal, blue and white china, and perhaps a vase filled with cabbage roses. The matching chairs and the windows might wear royal blue velvet, and the floor can be graced with a sapphire-hued Oriental carpet.

American and Scandinavian country kitchens and dining rooms share a love of painted wooden furniture, muted colors, ginghams, sprigged floral fabrics, and simple window treatments. American kitchen walls may be whitewashed or covered with a country floral or checked wallpaper, while the floor might be wood, terra-cotta tiles, or dimension stone. Blue highlights can include a display of antique tins and glassware, a braided rug, and cornflower blue countertops on blonde wood cabinets. In the Scandinavian kitchen, walls and furnishings are often painted pale blue, while the focal point of the room might be an armoire with rosemaling. A simple wooden table and chairs would be dressed in a gingham tablecloth and cushions, and the bleached wooden floor could be stenciled with blue and white checks and topped with a throw rug in one of the primary colors.

Both the American and Scandinavian country dining rooms might be outfitted with antique wooden tables and chairs; china cabinets full of blue and white porcelain, delftware, graniteware, or glassware; simple wrought-iron candlesticks; pale blue or cream painted walls; and lace panels on the windows. Suitable American country accessories include a blue and white patchwork quilt used as a tablecloth, stoneware crocks filled with wildflowers, and needlework samplers or folk art. Classic Scandinavian touches include an antique blue and white tiled stove, a curvaceous gilded standing clock, and a Swedish Rococo sideboard.

The sunny Mediterranean region is a magical place for alfresco dining and rustic, romantic decorating. The kitchen and dining areas are often combined in one open living space. White plaster walls are decorated with arches, native tiles, and azure woodwork and shutters. Furnishings include iron or black wooden tables, cabinets, and rush-seat chairs. Terra-cotta floors are topped with striped woven rugs, and accents such as turquoise and white ceramic pots filled with vibrant flowers and wooden bowls brimming with local produce grace the large, airy rooms.

In French country homes, kitchens commonly feature terra-cotta floors, whitewashed plaster walls with beamed ceilings, or walls done in petite floral or striped wallpapers. Work surfaces are often set with blue and

white tiles, and the wooden tables and chairs wear viva-
cious Provençal fabrics. Unique kitchen accoutrements include a panetière (vintage bread box), hanging copper
pans, wire baskets, and enamelware pitchers. Nearby
dining rooms enchant with their long wooden tables, rush-
seat chairs with carved floral designs, and elegant ar-
moires and china cabinets. Their terra-cotta floors contrast
nicely with blue floral rugs, and chandeliers and candles
illuminate the cream or white walls.

The contemporary kitchen or dining room offers both
style and convenience. You can choose from an endless
array of colorful cabinets, countertops, and appliances in
such hues as royal blue, cobalt, gray-blue, and teal. There
are also myriad ceramic tiles, lighting fixtures, flooring,
window and wall treatments, and textiles to choose from.
Contemporary kitchens and dining areas can be ultramod-
ern or an updated version of a traditional or regional
style. With a blue sky palette to pull it all together, you
can even mix and match elements from a variety of styles.

Right, top: THIS AMERICAN COUNTRY KITCHEN IS A CHARMING VISION IN
WHITE. THE RUNNER AND CHAIR CUSHION ADD RICH BLUE ACCENTS, WHILE THE
CABINETS, CANE-SEATED STOOL, WICKER CHAIR, AND WOODEN FLOOR ADD
TEXTURE. THE OWNERS' LOVE OF BARNYARD ANIMALS IS CELEBRATED IN THE
DISPLAY OF COLLECTIBLES ABOVE THE KITCHEN WINDOW.

Right, bottom: THIS WINE CONNOISSEUR'S KITCHEN SPEAKS FRENCH
COUNTRY THROUGH ITS DECORATIVE TILES, AS WELL AS ITS SPARKLING WHITE
CUPBOARDS, CHARMING BLUE GLASSES, AND BOUQUET OF FRESH FLOWERS.

Above, left: BY ITSELF, WHITE CAN SEEM COOL OR CLINICAL, BUT WHEN COMBINED WITH BLUE, IT CREATES A SENSE OF JOY, PURITY, AND SOPHISTICATION, AS IN THIS VIBRANT MEDITERRANEAN COUNTRY DINING ROOM AND KITCHEN. **Above, right:** THIS CONTEMPORARY KITCHEN ECHOES THE COUNTRY PENCHANT FOR BLUE AND WHITE CHECKS THROUGH ITS PLEASING TILED COUNTER, WALLS, AND ACCESSORIES. **Opposite:** COBALT BLUE COUNTERTOPS, YELLOW AND CORNFLOWER BLUE TILES, WARM WOOD, AND COLORFUL ACCESSORIES CREATE AN OUTGOING MOOD IN THIS CONTEMPORARY KITCHEN.

Opposite: DAZZLING "MAJOLICA BLUE" AND RED TILES ADORN THIS KITCHEN'S FLOOR AND WALLS. BEAMED STUCCO WALLS AND SIMPLE LIGHTING FIXTURES AND ACCESSORIES PROVIDE COUNTER- POINT TO THE ROOM'S FESTIVE PATTERNS AND HUES.

Right: VIBRANTLY COLORED SPANISH TILES SURROUNDING A VINTAGE BREAD OVEN ARE THE FOCAL POINT OF THIS MEXICAN COUNTRY KITCHEN. THE WHITE STUCCO WALLS, DEEP BLUE CABINETS, AND DECORATIVE CANISTERS ENHANCE THE ROOM'S CELESTIAL THEME.

Opposite: THE SHIMMERING MIDNIGHT BLUE FLOOR ENHANCES THE SERENE AMBIENCE OF THIS BREEZY MEDITERRANEAN COUNTRY DINING ROOM.

Above, left: ENTERTAINER DANNY KAYE ONCE SAID, "LIFE IS A GREAT BIG CANVAS." SO, TOO, ARE EACH OF THE ROOMS OF OUR HOMES, INCLUDING OUR OUTDOOR LIVING SPACES. THIS MEDITERRANEAN COURTYARD IS AN EXQUISITE ALFRESCO "PAINTING" THAT DELIGHTS THE EYE WITH RICH BLUE GLASSWARE, SPARKLING WHITE PLATES AND LINENS, LUXURIANT PINK BLOOMS, AND FRESH FRUITS IN A RAINBOW OF COLORS. **Above, right:** THE NEOCLASSICAL SHELL IS A POPULAR ARCHITECTURAL MOTIF IN MEDITERRANEAN-STYLE HOMES. THIS LUMINOUS BLUE WALL SHOWCASES A BUILT-IN DINING ROOM CUPBOARD WHERE A TREASURED COLLECTION OF CHINA IS DISPLAYED.

Above, left: COLLECTIONS SHOULD BE DISPLAYED AND ENJOYED, AS THIS KITCHEN HEARTILY ATTESTS. IN TRUE AMERICAN COUNTRY SPIRIT, WOODEN CABINETS AND EARTH-TONED TILES PROVIDE A WONDERFUL BACKDROP FOR DAZZLING BLUE AND WHITE DISHES AND GRANITEWARE, AS WELL AS A RUSTIC BASKET AND CHERISHED ROOSTER.

Above, right: THE CORNER OF THIS ROMANTIC FEDERAL DINING ROOM SPEAKS OF RELAXED ELEGANCE, THANKS TO CHECKERED CHAIR CUSHIONS, A BASKET OF FRESH FLOWERS, A MIX OF BLUE CHINA, AND A VINTAGE BLUE AND WHITE QUILT. **Opposite:** TIME STANDS STILL IN THIS FEDERAL-ERA DINING ROOM, WHICH IS GRACED WITH A LOVELY BAY WINDOW AND FIREPLACE. A VARIETY OF BLUES IS OFTEN FOUND IN SUCH A TRADITIONAL SETTING, FROM ETHEREAL SKY BLUE TO RICH ROYAL BLUE, AND EVEN THE GREEN-TINGED APOTHECARY BLUE, A PROMINENT HUE FOUND IN GEORGE WASHINGTON'S HOME AT MOUNT VERNON.

Ocean-Inspired Bedrooms and Bathrooms

It's de rigueur to decorate a bedroom and bath in the same serene maritime color scheme, perhaps even spotlighting boats, lighthouses, whales, or seashells in your decorating theme through wallpapers, fabrics, and accessories. Whatever design motif inspires you, blue and white should be used to color large areas of the bedroom and bath, such as walls, floors, window treatments, bed dressings, and bathroom fixtures.

Traditional bedrooms are outfitted with elaborate blue and white decors, while country and contemporary bedrooms are often decorated simply and sparingly. The bed and its accoutrements are usually the focal point of the decor in any bedroom. Federal and Regency bedrooms may feature a curvaceous neoclassical Empire sleigh bed, a four-poster bed with graceful turnings and a straight canopy, or a low "field" bed with an arched canopy. Traditional bed hangings often use up to sixty yards (55m) of such fabrics as indigo and white toile de Jouy or sapphire and cream chintz or silk, as well as summery cotton stripes or prints. In the Regency bedroom, white voile might be draped from a gilded corona above the bed. Delicate tables, chairs, chaise longues, and chests of drawers also furnish the room. The blue and white theme repeats in the striped or floral wallpaper, toile upholstery, and Aubusson carpets.

During the Victorian era, if a bedroom faced north, it was often decorated in a deep blue striped, floral, or foliage wallpaper, while a sunnier exposure called for pastel wallpapers in blues and whites. A typical Victorian bedroom can include a brass, iron, or wooden spool bed

Opposite: A GARDEN OF SENSUAL DELIGHTS, THIS BEDROOM INSPIRES A MOOD OF TRANQUILITY WITH ITS CASUAL MIX OF FORMAL AND WICKER FURNITURE, ITS COMFORTING BLUE AND WHITE QUILT, SOFT CARPETING, FRESH FLOWERS, AND THE MESMERIZING SIGHT, SOUND, AND FRAGRANCE OF THE OCEAN.

draped with a lace coverlet or a crazy quilt, a wooden floor covered with area rugs, an upholstered chair or settee, a night table with a stained glass or fringed period lamp, lace curtains, and several framed paintings or prints and knickknacks.

The American country bedroom provides blissful comfort with warm wood, woven wicker, or sturdy brass or wrought-iron furniture. Medium or deep blue and white accents can include heirloom patchwork quilts as well as hooked, braided, or rag rugs. Windows often wear

Above, left: Powder blue walls enhance the allure of this Regency-style bedroom's mural of ancient ruins. The antique dresser and framed artwork add to the room's historic ambience. **Above, right:** This teenager's retreat enchants with its American country mix of fabrics, flowers, warm wood, nautical paintings, old license plates, and a beloved childhood friend.

demure lace or sprigged floral curtains, which echo print wallpapers or stenciled borders. Country accessories include baskets full of blue wildflowers or blue glass bottles filled with daisies and forget-me-nots.

The Scandinavian country bedroom offers an even simpler interpretation of the soft celestial palette. The room charms with a cozy built-in bed or a freestanding wooden bed with a blue gingham, calico, or striped bedspread and matching bed and window curtains, ice blue walls with blue wooden shelves, bleached wooden floors with striped runners, and, for cheery contrast, a red or yellow painted chair.

A typical Mediterranean bedroom is a cool, white sanctuary. The room usually features whitewashed walls and wooden floorboards covered with sheepskin or woven rugs. Windows have muslin curtains or azure blue shutters. Furnishings may include a simple iron bed topped with a white crocheted comforter, a wooden cupboard for clothing, and a rush-seat chair. Accessories are kept simple, such as a decorative ceramic hand basin on the wall for a splash of color and a treasured painting or religious icon.

The French country bedroom is usually furnished with an elaborately carved armoire, a *lit bateau* (wooden boat bed) or a painted iron bed, and a wooden or wrought-iron chair and table. Windows might be veiled with net or lace curtains and a polished floor made cozy with a woven rug. In true Provençal tradition, walls are covered with layers of wallpaper and borders. Key wallpaper choices include fresh yellow and cobalt blue or dusty blue and white patterns such as miniature florals, trelliswork, dots, twigs and leaves, and ribbons. The wallpaper could be complemented by similar blue-hued patterns in the bed linens or accent pillows.

The contemporary bedroom has license to employ everything from the deepest to the most demure shades of blue and white, keeping in mind the golden design rule that "less is more." Midnight blue walls can make a large room seem cozy, while off-white walls with a pale azure ceiling will open up a small space. A restful ambience can be achieved with blue carpeting, wooden or metal furnishings, glass- or marble-topped tables, vertical blinds or Roman shades, recessed lighting, simple torchères, textured pillows, and a contemporary painting or two.

Today's half- or full bath can easily echo the decor of any bedroom by matching or using similar fabrics, wallpaper patterns, furnishings, and accessories. A variety of contemporary and reproduction products exist to outfit the bathroom, as many homeowners today want to transform their baths from strictly utilitarian spaces for bathing and grooming to luxurious retreats designed in a favorite period or regional style. Every color of the rainbow is available in today's selection of fixtures, flooring, wallpapers, ceramic tiles, and durable semigloss paints.

Opposite: THE SLATE BLUE WALLS AND WHITE BEDS AND LINENS OF THIS RETREAT PROVIDE COUNTERPOINT TO THE PROFUSION OF BOTANICAL DESIGNS IN THE FRAMED PRINTS, BEDSPREADS, AND UPHOLSTERED FURNITURE. **Above, left:** TAKING COLOR CUES FROM ITS RADIANT TILED FIREPLACE, THIS BEDROOM'S BLUE AND WHITE THEME IS IDEAL FOR ITS SUNNY SOUTHERN EXPOSURE. THE MEDIUM BLUES OF THE BEDSPREAD, WINDOW TREATMENTS, AND ARMCHAIR ADD A SENSE OF COOLNESS, AS DO THE WHITE DRESSERS, PALE BLUE WALLS, AND WHITE CEILING. **Above, right:** IT'S IMPORTANT TO REMEMBER THAT WHEN DECORATING WITH BLUE AND WHITE, THE SATURATION OR BRILLIANCE OF BOTH COLORS SHOULD MATCH TO CREATE A SENSE OF HARMONY. THE DUSTY BLUE OF THIS AMERICAN COUNTRY BEDROOM'S CURTAINS AND BEDSKIRTS BLENDS PERFECTLY WITH THE GRAY-BLUE RUG AND SERENE WHITE WALLS.

Left: This formal bedroom, filled with rich Federal-era furnishings, is bathed in natural light and fresh island breezes. The handsome shuttered doors and the quilt on the bed add a regal blue ambience to this shaded sanctuary.

Left: Often, today's American country rooms offer an eclectic blend of furnishings and accessories. This bedroom successfully mixes dark- and light-toned period furnishings with contemporary cornflower blue walls and a cream-colored ceiling. The room's black-framed botanical prints strike a modern chord, while the wooden floor, patchwork quilt, and braided rug celebrate tradition.

Opposite: A sea of blue floral carpet and Wedgwood blue and white fabric color this traditional bedroom. The Federal-era furnishings include a full-tester bed, a gracious high chest, and an elegant settee.

Left: THE SUN AND STARS PRESIDE OVER THIS FAIRYTALE-LIKE BEDROOM RETREAT. THE GRACE OF THE CLOUDS ON THE CEILING IS REFLECTED IN THE WISPY BLUE WINDOW DRAPERY. AN ANTIQUE ANGEL, SEVERAL RABBITS, A MINIATURE CHAIR, AND A VENERABLE METAL BED ADD TO THE MAGIC.

Below: Mediterranean country homes are commonly painted white, while their window frames and doors are resplendent in such vibrant shades of blue as turquoise, cobalt, or azure. Here, a vivid bedroom doorway opens onto a sunlit terrace.

Above: This lovely mirror doesn't need a fresh coat of paint. Its charm lies in its aged patina, which attests to years of faithful service in the pursuit of beauty. The bedroom's pastel blue walls, old-fashioned dresser with glass pulls, sea green tin wind-up alarm clock, and vase of blue hydrangeas also reflect simpler times.

Below: Glossy ceramic tiles in Wedgwood blue and indigo create a dramatic counterpoint to the white and blonde of the ceiling, floor, and tub surround. The color palette of this bathroom makes such a strong statement that few accessories are needed.

Above: This spacious bathroom retreat pampers with its contemporary bathtub in Stratosphere blue tiles, expansive cabinets, plush carpeting, and superb view of the great outdoors.

Opposite: In this elegant bathroom, the cabinet, oval mirror, ginger jars, and tiled floor suggest a Victorian mood, while the striped valances and formal side chair lend Regency flair. Cobalt blue glass tumblers and jars add a contemporary touch.

True-Blue Accessories

"A thing of beauty is a joy forever." When we think of the inner and outer beauty of our homes, John Keats' poetic words ring true. Even the little things add splendor, for treasured blue and white accessories paint our rooms with personality and, in many cases, a sense of history.

Whether we exhibit ginger jars on rustic dressers or display favorite plates and platters on the walls, blue and white china is a stellar accessory that's perfect for any decor. Between the 1500s and 1800s, spices, fabrics, and radiant blue and white porcelain were exported from Cathay (known today as China) to Europe and America, where only the wealthy could afford them. Around 1735, the process for making china was duplicated by potters in Meissen, Germany, and by 1750 the English were creating such enduring blue and white china patterns as Blue Willow, Canton, Fitzhugh, and Nanking. During the Victorian era, a great deal of blue and white china produced in Staffordshire, England, was exported to America, where it became a symbol of status. Another desirable accessory is antique flow blue china, produced primarily in England from the 1830s through 1910. Flow blue features a cobalt, navy, or steel blue underglaze that is slightly blurred from the firing process.

Luminous blue glass pitchers, vases, and candlesticks can also add immense charm to windowsills and tabletops in your home. One of many styles of collectible glassware is Depression glass, manufactured by numerous American companies between 1920 and 1940. Of the more than twenty-five colors made, common Depression glass hues include pink, green, and amber. Some less frequently manufactured colors are turquoise, peacock blue, ultramarine, cobalt, and ice blue—all sought after today for their beauty and rarity.

Hand-painted tiles are another vibrant way to introduce sea and sky colors to your favorite indoor and outdoor spaces. Tiles that are porous are sensitive to extreme cold and are unable to withstand water penetration, so you might use them around your fireplace and hearth.

Opposite: When displaying blue and white accessories, you can add visual punch by introducing vibrant yellow, orange, or red accents, such as the flowers on this kitchen dresser. Blue and white is a sociable duet that becomes even more appealing when highlighted with warm colors.

Tiles that are nonabsorbent are hard and able to withstand moisture and drastic temperature changes, so they make ideal sink backsplashes and garden pathways. Enchanting tiles to look for include blue and white delftware from Holland, turquoise or cobalt and white tiles from the Middle East, and blue majolica tiles from Italy, Portugal, Spain, and Mexico.

A symbol of thrift and creativity, the handmade American quilt is also partial to a blue and white palette. In the early 1800s, almost every American quiltmaker made at least one indigo and white quilt. The color combination was considered harmonious, and indigo dye's superior ability to withstand repeated washings had been renowned since the Colonial era, when indigo was the most widely used coloring agent for homespun fabrics. Several quilt patterns that are traditionally done in blue and white include Irish Chain, Feathered Star, Hole in a Barn Door, and Drunkard's Path.

Around the world, several stunning fabrics that were created centuries ago continue to inspire a variety of traditional and country-style blue and white pillows, curtains, tablecloths, wallpapers, and dinnerware. These include French toiles de Jouy, which feature single-color pastoral, Oriental, or historic scenes on a light ground; English glazed cotton chintzes bedecked with blossoms, ribbons, ivy, birds, and butterflies; and French Provençal cottons with tiny floral, geometric, or paisley patterns and sunny Mediterranean hues.

Today's toiles de Jouy were inspired by the copperplate fabrics designed by Christophe-Philippe Oberkampf, a Bavarian artisan who manufactured his decorative cotton-linen fabrics in Jouy-en-Josas, France, in the late eighteenth century. Chintz is frequently associated with English country decor, but it actually originated in India, where artisans lovingly created hand-painted or hand-blocked cotton and linen fabrics. These flora and fauna fabrics have been exported to Europe since the seventeenth century. Like chintz, the captivating fabrics that we associate with Provence today take their inspiration and motifs from the handmade prints that originated in India centuries ago. For more than two hundred years, vivid Provençal "Indienne" fabrics have been woven and printed in Tarascon, France, to emulate the unforgettable beauty of the landscape of southern France.

Another classic accessory that is often found in French and American country decors is graniteware, also known as enamelware or agate ware. Examples of graniteware include such utilitarian items as water pitchers, coffeepots, and canisters that were made of cast iron or sheet metal and coated with enamel. Alluring blue and white designs included swirls, checks, stripes, speckles, floral motifs, windmills, and sailboats. From the late 1800s through 1940, graniteware was produced throughout Europe and America. Blue and white graniteware is very popular among collectors today, for in the antique business blue apparently attracts more buyers than other colors.

Legendary artist Pablo Picasso once said, "Why do two colors put next to one another sing?" When you lavish your home with blue and white furnishings and accessories, you can see and feel the perfect harmony to which Picasso referred. The boldest or softest blues and whites enchant us, reflecting our enduring love of the sea, the sky, and the precious blooms of our gardens.

Below, left: Whether you display old blue glass bottles, contemporary vases, or several Depression glass pitchers on your windowsill, when the sun breaks through your collection will sparkle like sapphires. **Below, right:** Drunkard's Path is a beloved classic quilt pattern for good reason. Simple blocks—each is a square cut diagonally in half by a semicircle—in just two colors create a striking and seemingly complex design. This beautiful example certainly deserves its place of honor on the wall.

Above, left: THIS CLOSE-UP OF A SCANDINAVIAN COUNTRY LIVING ROOM WALL DEPICTS A PAINTING WITHIN A PAINTING. THE LOVELY SEASIDE SKETCH IS ENCIRCLED BY A HAND-STENCILED WALL, A TIME-HONORED ALTERNATIVE TO WALLPAPER. **Above, right:** REMINISCENT OF NINETEENTH-CENTURY FLOW BLUE CHINA, THIS DELICATE DINNERWARE OFFERS WINSOME FLORAL DESIGNS THAT ARE COMPLEMENTED BY THE BUTTERFLY TABLECLOTH AND SPRINGTIME GRAPE HYACINTHS.

Opposite: LIKE A SUMPTUOUS STILL-LIFE PAINTING, THIS ALFRESCO TABLE SETTING MESMERIZES WITH ITS COBALT GLASS DINNERWARE, SILVER AND CRYSTAL ACCESSORIES, COMPLEMENTARY BLUE FABRICS, AND LUSH GARDEN PLANTS.

Opposite: A CASUAL BLEND OF SEVERAL BLUE AND WHITE FABRICS AND WALL COVERINGS CAN LOOK SPLENDID IN ANY DECOR WHEN THE INTENSITY OF THE BLUES MATCH. HERE, SEVERAL MEDIUM BLUE PLAID, GINGHAM, AND TOILE DE JOUY ACCESSORIES SING IN HARMONY. **Below:** IN MANY SCANDINAVIAN COUNTRY KITCHENS, BLEACHED WOODEN FLOORS ARE STAINED OR PAINTED WITH A BLUE AND WHITE CHECKERBOARD MOTIF FOR ADDED COLOR AND DESIGN.

Above: A CLOSE LOOK AT THIS COUNTRY BEDROOM'S CHECKED DRAPES REVEALS THEIR REVERSIBLE FLORAL THEME, AS WELL AS AN IDYLLIC PASTORAL VIEW FROM THE WINDOW.

Above, left: An antique blue and white tiled stove takes center stage in the drawing room of this Swedish pavilion. The elegant chair beside the stove dates from the rule of Gustav III of Sweden in the eighteenth century, when furnishings had soft, fluid lines and their painted surfaces reflected natural light. Such furnishings emulated the decorative French Rococo style. **Above, right:** The versatility of paint and the vitality of blue and white shine through in this home's hand-painted faux tile floor border, designed to echo the wall's real tiles and the decorative table. **Left:** As building blocks of the French country kitchen, these decorative tiles deliver practical and pretty architectural verve with a classic floral motif.

Right: BLUE AND WHITE
PORCELAIN IS PERENNIALLY POPULAR
BECAUSE IT COMES IN SEVERAL
VIBRANT SHADES OF BLUE,
BLENDS WELL WITH BOTH WARM
AND COOL COLORS, AND IS
UNMISTAKABLY CLASSY.

Part Four
Stone & Marble

INTRODUCTION

Stone evokes many moods in the home. Strong and earthy, stone proclaims substance, permanence, and stability. In architecture, it recalls the relative safety and security of caves, our primordial homes built into mountains and hillsides.

From the pyramids of ancient Egypt to the medieval castles of Europe, stone figures prominently in the cultural and design history of Western civilization. Almost three millennia before the birth of Christ, the Egyptian pyramids were constructed in the desert like abstract man-made mountains. Originally sheathed in smooth white limestone, these kingly tombs reflected the blinding radiance of the desert sun. Visually, they connected the earth with the sky. Symbolically, they linked Pharaoh, the entombed ruler, with the sun god, Re, and immortality.

By the end of the sixth century B.C., the Greek temple became a dominant form in Western architecture. Raised on a platform, the typical temple housed an image of a victorious deity or sometimes an oracle in a *cella* (chamber) surrounded by rows of columns. The earliest temples were built of timber and sun-dried clay tiles, followed by temples of ashlar or hewn stone. By 525 B.C., the Greeks made temples out of local marble, which could be polished to a shine and carved with detailed scenes that were then painted. The public, barred from entering the *cella*, saw their temples from the outside only— as ranks of massive, weight-bearing columns supporting a heavy, ornamented roof. Ancient temple ruins still assert their dignity and authority over the rocky terrain of modern Greece.

During the eleventh century A.D., the Normans began building rocky fortifications, a Roman custom that had waned some four hundred years earlier. Stone was the dominant building material because it was strong, fireproof, versatile, and impenetrable. Stone castles, frequently situated on hilltops for passive defense, had slit windows and battlements to allow soldiers while in the relative safety of the fortifications to rain arrows on an approaching enemy.

A key building material for thousands of years, stone falls into three groups: igneous, sedimentary, and metamorphic. Igneous rock, such as granite and basalt, is formed by the solidification of magma (molten rock)

Opposite: The classical motifs carved into this gray and white marble mantel complement the small stone sculptures standing on top of it. Tall vases filled with lilies set at either end of the mantelpiece accentuate the creamy, light color of the marble and give the arrangement a look of elegant formality.

sandstone and limestone run the gamut from off white, gold, and gray to purple and pink. Limestone is a traditional building material in many parts of North America and Europe, and it is often used for flooring and garden walkways as rock that has been subjected to and changed by tremendous heat or pressure. Marble comes in myriad colors and has been a favorite of architects for centuries, although today it is most often used to lend a sense of elegance to interiors.

within the earth. Granite is tough, lasting, and weather- and water-resistant; it ranges in color from black to white, gray, and red. Granite is popular for use both outside and inside the home, where it appears on kitchen counters and backsplashes, fireplace mantels, and even bathroom tiles. Basalt can be blue, green, brown, or black. Sedimentary rocks, such as sandstone and limestone, are formed by the erosion of various substances. Sandstone is made from the sediment of eroded igneous stones, and limestone from shells and skeletons. The colors of

The fashion for stone has ebbed and flowed through the centuries. In recent years, however, we've witnessed a renewed interest in the use of stone and marble both inside and outside the home. These materials can be quite expensive, so often they are used only on the facade or in small but significant details such as mantels, doorways, and window frames. Today, stone or marble decorative items such as tables and countertops bespeak the home-owner's desire for substance and style. Whimsical applications for stone and marble are evident in contemporary design, which takes a fresh look at old motifs and uses them in new ways.

Above: SEVEN OF THE ORIGINAL THIRTY-EIGHT FLUTED DORIC COLUMNS SURVIVE IN THE TEMPLE OF APOLLO AT CORINTH, WHICH WAS BUILT CIRCA 540 B.C. INDIVIDUALLY CARVED CAPITALS, COVERED IN A MARBLE-DUST STUCCO SKIN, TOPPED THE COLUMNS, WHICH SUPPORTED AN ENTABLATURE AND PITCHED ROOF. ORIGINALLY, BRIGHT RED AND BLUE PAINTS WOULD HAVE HEIGHTENED THE TEMPLE'S DECORATIVE APPEAL.

Above: LIGHT AND SHADOW ADD DRAMA TO THIS TROPICAL SETTING. THE LOGGIA, OPEN BUT PROTECTED FROM THE ELEMENTS, RELIES ON THE COARSE STONE WALLS

OF THE HOUSE AND THE GENTLY TEXTURED STONE PATIO TO CREATE A RUSTIC RETREAT FROM THE HOT MIDDAY SUN.

—

FIRST IMPRESSIONS

A well-designed stone facade gives a house an aura of permanence, beauty, and stability. When made from locally quarried material, a stone facade can also tie a building into its immediate surroundings and geographic region. Local stone also has the advantage of costing less to transport to nearby building sites than imported stone.

The practice of using stone from nearby quarries is a very old one that still prevails today. The ancient Greeks patronized local quarries to construct their marble temples in the sixth century B.C. In the nineteenth and twentieth centuries, New York City architects built traditional brownstone townhouses of sandstone from quarries in New York state.

Old fieldstone farmhouses are abundant in rural Pennsylvania, while suburban housing developments in

the area maintain regional character with local fieldstone facing. This thin stone veneer applied to concrete block or frame construction evokes a rural feeling and gives the look of stone without the cost.

The English are masters of stone construction, and their talents are nowhere more apparent than in the hilly Cotswolds. This region of England includes Gloucestershire and parts of Avon, Warwickshire, and Worcester. Cottages, manors, palaces, and whole villages built of this indigenous limestone warm the landscape with their tawny hues. Indeed, this ubiquitous golden stone brings harmony and an enduring allure to the region. Different building stones come from other parts of Great Britain, including granite from Cornwall and flint from East Anglia.

Opposite: A flagstone floor, stucco walls painted golden yellow, and coarse stone trim around the door create a warm, sunny, informal courtyard setting. Planters and window boxes filled with annuals, climbing roses, a tiny bed of purple and blue delphiniums, and a comfortable rustic chair animate this cheerful scene. **Above:** Stone columns and a sculpture stained with age form the perfect backdrop for colorful garden plants. Old stone softens the contrast between the climber's scarlet blooms and the purple-flowering shrubs. Lush green foundation plants look perfectly natural jumbled against the rugged stone walls.

Slate, another popular building material, is found around the world, including Canada, the United States, Europe, and Africa. Slate splits easily into thin slices. It is also hard, fine grained, and weather-resistant, making it an excellent choice for roofing tiles, wall shingles, and outdoor paths. Its various colors include gray, red, blue, olive, and light and dark green.

Sometimes only part of a facade is made of stone. A Palladian stone portico adds grandeur and formality to a building. It designates a formal entrance, especially in large dwellings where lesser entries are intentionally plain and do not attract attention. Stone trim enhances windows, doors, corners, rooflines, and outdoor stairways. Stone looks particularly attractive when it contrasts with surrounding building materials, such as red brick or painted stucco.

Stone persists outdoors. It lasts best, however, when used in a climate similar to the one where it was quarried. Unlike wood, concrete, and many other outdoor building materials, stone doesn't require painting or exterior finishes. Limestone facades need occasional cleaning, since

Above: ALONG WITH WOOD, TWO TYPES OF STONE MAKE UP THE FACADE OF THIS COUNTRY HOUSE, WHICH BLENDS NATURALLY INTO THE SURROUNDING LANDSCAPE. THE FACADE'S NEAR SYMMETRY ACCENTUATES THE PERCEPTION OF STABILITY CREATED BY AN ABUNDANCE OF STONE. EXAGGERATED STONE TRIM BRINGS LEVITY TO THIS RATHER STAID BUILDING. A RETAINING WALL THAT FORMS A TRANSITION BETWEEN THE LAWN AND THE DRIVE EXTENDS THE EARTHY IMPACT OF STONE INTO THE GARDEN.

heavy urban pollution and extreme weather conditions affect its appearance. To avoid leaks, exterior stonework also needs repointing when the mortar between individual stones decays. Local stone weathers well, mellowing with time and improving with age.

Marble has endured as an outdoor building material for thousands of years in the mild climate of Greece, but it cannot withstand the harsh climatic changes of northern countries. Still, marble is popular in cooler countries as an elegant addition to transitional areas, such as entrance halls and courtyards. Generous expanses of marble flooring can form a graceful segue from the rough, natural textures of the outdoors to the softer, more decorative surfaces of a home's interior. Even a small marble piece, such as a marble-topped table or console, can lend sophistication to a transitional space. Whether employed as the main building materials of a home or used simply as decorative accents, stone and marble create a sense of permanence and ageless beauty wherever they are used.

Above: TALL, CAREFULLY SHAPED EVERGREENS LINE THE MAIN PATH TO THIS HOUSE IN THE COTSWOLD VILLAGE OF ARLINGTON. THE TALL, FLAT-TOPPED TREES TOWERING OVER THE GARDEN WALL ECHO THE IMPOSING SYMMETRY OF THE ROOF'S TWIN GABLES. MOREOVER, THE ALTERNATION OF LIGHT STONE AND DARK FOLIAGE CREATES A VISUAL RHYTHM THAT CARRIES THE GAZE STRAIGHT TO THE FRONT DOOR, THE FOCUS OF THE FACADE.

Below: Bright blue painted trim brings gaiety to the limestone facade of this house. The feeling of whimsy and spontaneity is heightened by a dooryard garden filled with a jumble of pink and white foxgloves and large-leafed hollyhocks, both traditional cottage garden flowers. Opposite: The simple gray limestone facade of this farmhouse suits the informal landscape surrounding it. Exuberant wisteria spreads over one end of the house, linking the austere structure to its natural setting.

Above: The peculiar charm of this modest Cotswold house derives from its harmonious facade, which is composed of indigenous golden limestone set off by ebullient landscaping in green and a range of hot magenta hues. Because of an apparently inexhaustible supply of Cotswold limestone, palaces, manors, and village dwellings in the region are built of this popular and attractive rock.

Opposite: MASSIVE IN SCALE, AN IMPOSING PALLADIAN PORTICO WITH FOUR COLUMNS AND A STONE PEDIMENT CONTAINING AN OCULUS (ROUND OPENING) IS CENTRAL TO THE DESIGN OF THIS GRAND AND STATELY BUILDING. BY PROJECTING THE PORTICO OUT FROM THE MAIN STRUCTURE, THE ARCHITECT HAS INCREASED ITS IMPORTANCE AND ENHANCED THE DRAMA OF LIGHT AND SHADOW ON THE FACADE.

Above: STONE BECOMES A THEME THAT INTEGRATES THE INTERIOR OF THIS ELEGANT BUILDING WITH THE EXTERIOR. IN THE ENTRANCE HALL, THE STONE FLOOR LOOKS GLOSSY WITH AGE AND WEAR. STONE FLOORS STAND UP WELL TO INDOOR USE IN HIGH-TRAFFIC AREAS. THE DOORWAY COMBINES DIFFERENT HUES OF STONE—GRAY FOR THE STEP, IVORY FOR THE CAPITALS, AND SOFT GOLD FOR THE PILASTERS. PLANTS IN CONTRASTING SHADES OF GREEN ENLIVEN THE HOME'S CLASSICAL STONE FACADE AND GRAVELED COURTYARD.

Opposite: DECORATED WITH A COLLECTION OF ARCHITECTURAL FRAGMENTS AND A ROW OF BUSTS ON PEDESTALS, THIS GRACEFUL LOGGIA PROVIDES AN ESCAPE FROM THE HEAT OF THE DAY. THE LOGGIA, THE FRAGMENTS, AND THE BUSTS AND PEDESTALS ARE ALL MADE OF STONE, WHICH PROVIDES THE UNIFYING ELEMENT IN THIS SETTING. LAVISH, DROOPY VINES HANGING FROM THE TERRACE ABOVE SOFTEN THE FORMAL REGULARITY OF THE ARCADE. **Below:** VINES OVERRUN THIS GOTHIC RUIN, WHICH BEARS A MESSAGE IN ITS TRANSIENT BEAUTY: CIVILIZATIONS FADE, BUILDINGS CRUMBLE, AND TIME CONQUERS THE CONQUERORS. BECAUSE OF STONE'S DURABILITY, HOWEVER, THIS TRACERY HAS SURVIVED FOR SEVERAL HUNDRED YEARS.

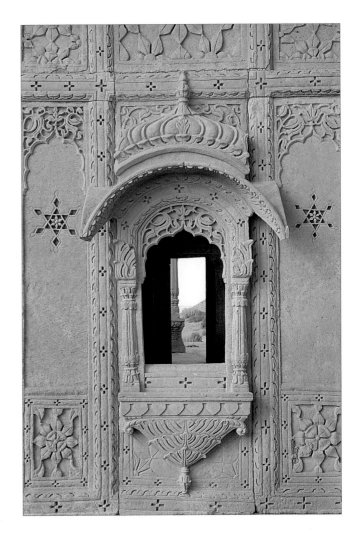

Above: THIS SANDSTONE WINDOW BELONGS TO THE TOMBS OF KINGS AT BADA BAGH NEAR JAISALMER, INDIA. IT IS A FINE EXAMPLE OF THE STONE CARVER'S ART. STYLIZED NATURALISTIC DESIGNS CUT IN BOTH HIGH AND LOW RELIEF ENHANCE THE PLAY OF LIGHT AND SHADOW ON THE TOMB'S SURFACE.

Above: The white stone walls and trim of this Italian villa reflect the warmth of the sun. Small round windows, known as oculi, form a band under the roof. Rounded stone pediments and carved shells cap French doors, which open onto small balconies. Lush green palms and bougainvillea, a scrambling woody vine with brilliant purple bracts, paint a picture of sultry splendor, especially when contrasted with the white facade and cloudless blue sky.

Opposite: Framed by palm fronds, a stunning view awaits visitors to the stone terrace at Villa Tritone in Sorrento, Italy. The busts on staggered posts represent forebears, signifying an ancient lineage and the connection between present and past. Like their Roman ancestors, urban Italian aristocrats built villas to retreat from hectic city lives into the peaceful existence of the countryside.

Left: An intricately carved stone doorway lies on the main axis of this villa's facade. Symmetrically placed palms and a central fountain in a rectangular reflecting pool reinforce this line of sight. The smooth white stucco walls of the building help cool the interior by reflecting the intense sunlight. **Above:** The simplicity of the smooth stone facade of this villa makes the architectural details of the building even more dramatic. A French door framed by an extremely tall Gothic arch opens onto a delicate latticed stone balcony. A gracefully twisting stone staircase punctuated with carved stone finials leads up to the massive front door.

Opposite: THE STONE ENTRANCE HALL OF THIS CASTLE EXUDES ELEGANCE. ITS COOL, NEUTRAL COLOR PROVIDES THE PERFECT BACKDROP FOR AN ELABORATE BLACK WROUGHT-IRON BALUSTRADE AND AN IMPOSING LIGHT FIXTURE OF THE SAME MATERIAL. A GLEAMING BRASS HANDRAIL AND SUNBEAMS PLAYING ON SMOOTH STONE SURFACES ADD DYNAMIC CONTRAST TO THE SETTING.

Below: THE SIMPLICITY OF PALE, UNADORNED STRIPED WALLS OFFSETS THE STRONG COLOR AND PATTERN OF THE TWO-TONE POLISHED MARBLE FLOOR IN THIS HALLWAY. THE PATTERN OF WHITE DIAMONDS EXTENDING FROM ROOM TO ROOM UNIFIES THE CONNECTING ROOMS AND DRAWS THE GAZE FROM ONE ROOM TO THE NEXT.

Above: A STYLIZED WAVE MOTIF IS THE SUBJECT OF THE DECORATIVE MOSAIC BELOW THE CHAIR RAIL IN THIS GRACIOUS ENTRYWAY. MADE OF SMALL STONE SQUARES IN DIFFERENT COLORS, THE DESIGN IS EMBEDDED IN MORTAR TO HOLD IT IN PLACE. ALTHOUGH THIS PATTERN IS SIMPLE, SOME MOSAICS HAVE THE COMPLEXITY AND RICHNESS OF FINE PAINTINGS. TRAVERTINE TILES COVER THE WALL UNDER THE BORDER AND PAVE THE FLOOR.

Gathering Spots

In the family gathering areas of a home—living rooms, great rooms, family rooms, dining rooms, and kitchens—stone and marble can create a sense of coziness or of formality. At once earthy and sophisticated, these durable materials can be used to make stylish walls, hearths, floors, counters, and columns.

In a cottage, a rustic stone hearth can be cozy and intimate, while in a larger home, a carved stone mantel brings elegance and stability to the design. Rustic walls made of indigenous stone give communal living spaces a picturesque, natural appeal by creating a direct link between indoors and out. Walls of gleaming polished granite, travertine, or marble, on the other hand, form a

striking formal backdrop for art objects and add purity and calmness to a design scheme.

Load-bearing pillars of stone can replace interior walls in the social rooms. Pillars open up indoor space and allow circulation, making it easier to entertain large groups. These pillars or columns can seem formal in a living room, when given a lintel and proper entablature, or casual in a great room or family room, where stone stands up to the wear and tear of children, pets, and parties.

It makes good sense to install stone floors in public areas that get lots of traffic because stone wears well. Stone also makes it easy to wipe up spills, and only water and a sponge or mop are needed to clean away dirt.

Opposite: There are two ways to install a sink in a stone surface. In this case, a stainless steel sink has been set into a polished granite work top. This method requires cutting appropriate holes by means of templates. Then the edge of each hole must be ground and polished to look like the main surface of the countertop. In the other, less expensive method, the sink sits on top of the hole, eliminating the need for finishing the edges of the opening. **Above:** This luxurious look is created with taupe speckled granite, dark walnut-stained wood, and brass fixtures. The gleaming brass and light, polished granite reflect the sunlight coming through the small-paned windows. These reflective materials balance the visual weight of the dark wood. In contrast to the gleaming brass and granite, the cabinets have the rich elegance of antique furniture.

Decorative stone floors take many forms. They can be inlaid with stone in different hues to create the effect of an area rug against a solid colored background. A geometric pattern of black granite against a backdrop of beige travertine makes a simple but striking design. It's also possible to incorporate color and complexity into walls or floors with mosaics. These small squares of colored stone or marble can be laid to form patterns or pictures. Mosaic floors or walls can give a room a sense of antiquity.

The kitchen is the heart of the home, a living space for family and friends. Here, stone and marble stand out for their practicality. In the kitchen, a rough, natural stone floor of slate or blue limestone gives the room a rustic character. Slate, moreover, is easy to clean and impervious to water. Cold, smooth marble is an excellent surface for pastry making, while thick, polished slabs of granite make superb, scratch-free work tops. Used together, stone and wood produce a snug, comfortable environment. Stone works like a magnet to draw people together and create a natural gathering place.

Moreover, plain slate, stone, or marble floors look good in most decorating situations. Stone or slate flooring with strong, graphic patterns or bold colors can add elegance to a room, and work best when the rest of the decor is kept sleek and simple.

Above: PRACTICAL YET ELEGANT, POLISHED GRANITE SUITS MOST KITCHEN DECORS. THIS HIGH-TECH CONTEMPORARY KITCHEN HAS SLEEK COUNTERS OF POLISHED GRAY GRANITE, WHICH COMPLEMENT THE BRUSHED STEEL OF THE STOVE AND DISHWASHER. WHITE LAMINATE CABINETS AND SHINY CHROME APPLIANCES COMPLETE THE DECOR.

Opposite: WHEN DECORATING WITH STONE, YOU DON'T HAVE TO LIMIT YOURSELF TO ONE TYPE OR COLOR. THE KITCHEN SHOWN HERE HAS A SLICK, GEOMETRICALLY PATTERNED STONE FLOOR AND BACKSPLASH. THEY ARE OF A SIMILAR, HARMONIOUS DESIGN BUT ARE NOT IDENTICAL. PATTERNED STONE FLOORS LIKE THE ONE PICTURED HERE WORK BEST WHEN THEY DON'T COMPETE WITH CLASHING PATTERNS AND COLORS. BEYOND THE KITCHEN, A FIREPLACE MADE OF ROUGH STONE AND THICK MORTAR HAS AN ALTOGETHER DIFFERENT, RUSTIC APPEARANCE.

Opposite: This stone-topped cooking alcove sparkles with wit and sophistication. The contrast between the traditional carved mantel and the stainless steel oven set beneath it would capture the imagination of even the most jaded visitor. **Above:** In this kitchen, polished black granite with white flecks has been used for the counters and backsplash. The dramatic granite blends with pale yellow walls, blond wooden cabinets, and abundant glass for a sophisticated effect. Rustic stone flooring adds a rustic element to the sleek design.

Opposite: NATURAL MATERIALS BRING THIS SLEEK, PRACTICAL KITCHEN DOWN TO EARTH. IN MANY HOMES, THE KITCHEN IS NOT JUST FOR COOKING BUT ALSO FOR SOCIALIZING AND DINING. DESIGNING WITH NATURAL MATERIALS LIKE THE HONEY-COLORED WOOD AND POLISHED GRANITE SHOWN HERE AVOIDS THE STERILE LOOK THAT MAKES SOME KITCHENS LESS THAN WELCOMING.

Above: MARBLE HAS TRADITIONALLY BEEN FAVORED FOR MAKING PASTRY BECAUSE OF ITS COLD SURFACE. MARBLE IS POROUS AND RELATIVELY SOFT, HOWEVER, SO IT STAINS EASILY. THE KEY TO SUCCESS WITH MARBLE AS A GENERAL WORK SURFACE IS WIPING UP SPILLED LIQUIDS QUICKLY AND USING A CUTTING BOARD FOR CHOPPING AND SLICING, SINCE THOSE ACTIVITIES CAN DESTROY THE FINISH OF A BEAUTIFUL MARBLE COUNTER SUCH AS THIS.

Right: SUNLIGHT SATURATES THIS KITCHEN, WHICH FEATURES A DESIGN THAT GLOWS WITH WARMTH. STAINED WOOD AND GLASS ARE THE PREVALENT MATERIALS, BUT THE THICK GRANITE TABLETOPS IN TAWNY PINK, BLACK, AND WHITE ADD TO THE SENSUOUS, ORGANIC QUALITY OF THE ROOM.

Opposite: Huge boulders form one wall of this extraordinary dining room. Chairs upholstered in leather, a long plank table, and a handsome Native American vessel fill the tight enclosure, creating a sophisticated interpretation of an indigenous Southwestern cave dwelling.

Above: Informality is the keynote of this living room dominated by a sturdy fireplace of coarse stones. Knotty pine floorboards, black wicker furniture, and a mantel, ceiling beams, and corner joints made of peeled logs complete the rustic spirit of this room.

Left: AN ANTIQUE CARVED STONE FIREPLACE ACCENTUATES THIS ROOM'S TRADITIONAL

FURNISHINGS. DARK PANELED WALLS, AN ORIENTAL CARPET, SEVERAL OLD TRUNKS USED

AS TABLES, AND A HUNTING PRINT ABOVE THE FIREPLACE PROVIDE CONTRASTING LUXURIOUS

TEXTURES AND ACT AS EMBLEMS OF THE GOOD LIFE. **Above:** SUNLIGHT POURS

THROUGH THE OPEN DOOR OF THIS DELIGHTFUL GREEN AND CREAM KITCHEN. A RUSTIC

STONE FLOOR, SIMPLE PAINTED CABINETS, RUSH SEATED LADDER-BACK CHAIRS, AND A

LONG PLANK TABLE CREATE A CLEAN COUNTRY LOOK.

Above: A MARBLE FIREPLACE FORMS THE CENTER OF THIS TRADITIONAL LIVING ROOM. THE PLAIN DESIGN OF THE FIREPLACE, ITS PALE GRAY AND WHITE HUES, AND ITS COOL, BROAD EXPANSE SERVE AS AN INDISPENSABLE COUNTERBALANCE TO THIS BUSY ARRANGEMENT OF PAINTINGS, ART OBJECTS, TERRA-COTTA POTS, MAHOGANY FURNISHINGS, AND A COUCH UPHOLSTERED IN BRILLIANT GREEN AND YELLOW.

Above: A TRADITIONAL CARVED MARBLE FIREPLACE BRINGS SUBSTANCE, STABILITY, AND ELEGANCE TO THIS AUSTERE BUT FORMAL INTERIOR. THE DECOR RELIES MORE ON NEUTRAL COLORS AND EARTHY MATERIALS THAN ON FANCY DECORATIONS FOR IMPACT. THE DRAMATICALLY TALL WINDOW LETS IN PLENTY OF SUNLIGHT AND A VIEW OF VERDANT TREES AND SHRUBS.

Above: This unusual table, comprised of individual stone blocks on a metal base, resembles a cobbled street. The coarse surface, accentuated by the fissures between the blocks, enlivens an otherwise plain seating area by introducing an element of the unexpected. **Opposite:** A wall of glass and a wall of stone serve to bring the outdoors inside this spacious living room. The pale stone used for the fireplace and surround adds to the light, airy feeling of the space, while the neutral palette and understated decor allow the striking view to be the main attraction.

Below: THE STONE FIREPLACE ADDS WELCOME TEXTURE TO THIS CASUAL, EASTERN-INSPIRED LIVING ROOM WITHOUT DISTRACTING ATTENTION FROM THE DRAMATIC PLANTS AND ART OBJECTS FILLING THE SPACE. **Opposite:** AN UNPAINTED STONE WALL ACCENTUATES THE FACT THAT THIS LOFT IS SEPARATE FROM THE LARGER SPACE, WHERE THE OTHER HALF OF THE SAME WALL IS PAINTED YELLOW. TAKEN TOGETHER, THE LOFT WALL, THE UNFINISHED WOOD FLOORS, AND THE PLAIN RAILINGS ENHANCE THE SIMPLE, RURAL DECOR.

Above: THE SENSUAL APPEAL OF THIS CONTEMPORARY LIVING ROOM COMES NOT FROM ITS COOL GRAY COLORS AND SIMPLE SHAPES BUT FROM THE CONTRAST OF TEXTURES. THE DEEP UPHOLSTERED ARMCHAIR COVERED IN A SOFT WOOL BLANKET LOOKS WARM AND INVITING, WHILE A VERTICAL STONE SCULPTURE AND TWO SIDE TABLES, BOTH CUBES OF COLD STONE, MAKE A DRAMATIC COUNTERPOINT TO THE WARM HARDWOOD FLOOR AND WOVEN GRASS RUG.

PRIVATE SPACES

Bedrooms and bathrooms are intimate places where we can relax and escape from the pressures of the world outside. Whether the decor you choose is lush and filled with creature comforts or spare and simply furnished, these rooms should inspire a sense of peace and harmony.

Bedrooms serve many functions, from the purely practical requirement for a sleeping space to the spiritual need for a place to dream. Stone and marble can be used to enhance the calm, soothing environment of the bedroom. Fireplaces are spots where a small amount of marble or stone can make a huge impact. In an elegant neoclassical home, marble surrounds and mantels can be carved into graceful motifs from the classical period, such as garlands, Greek keys, and eagles. In a country-style home, river rock or rough, quarried stone can add to the rustic ambience.

If you aren't lucky enough to have a fireplace, there are plenty of other ways to incorporate these timeless materials into the bedroom. Dressers and vanities can be topped with marble or granite, or a small table with a marble base can be added. Antique stores and flea markets often have pieces of architectural salvage that can make wonderful table bases. In the bedroom, a little stone or marble adds a lot of style.

In the bath, stone and marble have myriad applications because they are easy to clean and promote excellent sanitary conditions. Granite, marble, and slate tiles, which are available in many sizes and shapes, are wonderful for lining a shower stall or creating a tub surround. Some people choose to do the entire bathroom in stone, treating even the counters, walls, and floors with the rugged material. Limestone can

Opposite: HEAVY STONE WALLS PAINTED LINEN WHITE AND A LOW CEILING WITH EXPOSED BEAMS CREATE A COZY CAVELIKE FEELING IN THIS SMALL BEDROOM. TO INCREASE THE FEELING OF SPACE IN CLOSE QUARTERS, THE SAME OFF-WHITE COLOR IS USED FOR THE CURTAINS AND THE BEDSPREAD. **Above:** GLEAMING DARK BROWN MARBLE STREAKED WITH GRAY FITS PERFECTLY INTO THIS BATHROOM, WHERE THE FOCUS IS ON WORKS OF ART AND NOT ON THE CABINETS OR FIXTURES. HERE, THE DARK MARBLE DRAWS THE ATTENTION AWAY FROM ITSELF AND DIRECTS IT TOWARD THE OBJECTS IN THE ROOM.

be a beautiful choice, with its subtle blues and grays, but it is porous and therefore needs to be treated with a sealant before use.

Anything goes where color is concerned. Glossy black granite or cool white marble can be set off with minimalist chrome and glass fixtures and accessories for a sleek, sophisticated look. Warm taupe or beige travertine combines with shiny brass fixtures and dark wood cabinetry to lend an aura of traditional refinement to the bath. Marble and granite in rich reds and greens can heighten a mood of sensuousness and luxury. Even a rustic, old-world ambience can be created with these materials: choose slate or marble in earthy browns and beiges, or soft golden limestone with a weathered finish.

Above:. A RUGGED STONE WALL MAKES A DRAMATIC STATEMENT IN THIS ECLECTIC BEDROOM. NICHES HAVE BEEN CUT INTO THE WALL TO PROVIDE A PLACE FOR BOOKS, ELIMINATING THE NEED FOR A NIGHTSTAND. THE RICH DAMASK BED LINENS AND CURTAINS AND THE ORIENTAL RUG ADD A SENSE OF WARMTH AND LUXURY THAT COMPLEMENTS THE RUSTIC NATURE OF THE STONE AND STUCCO WALLS. **Opposite:** A CENTRAL LEADED-GLASS ROSE WINDOW SET INTO A GRAND ARCH CREATES A DRAMATIC FOCAL POINT FOR THIS BEDROOM. THE ARCH, FILLED WITH EXPOSED BRICK, HAS TWO MARBLE INSETS SYMMETRICALLY PLACED ON EITHER SIDE OF THE CIRCLE.

Opposite: This light, elegant bathroom has a full marble shower stall, marble wainscoting, and a marble floor. All the edges in the room, including the chair rail, have been ground to a rounded finish for both practical and aesthetic reasons. **Above:** Dark colors tend to shrink a room, but you can counteract this effect in different ways. In this bathroom, for example, the dark green marble walls and tub surround have a polished surface that is reflective even in low light situations. A tall mirror to one side of the tub reflects not just the available light but also the opposite side of the room, which makes the space appear larger.

Below: THIS TRAVERTINE TUB AREA LOOKS BEAUTIFUL BUT REQUIRES SPECIAL CARE. TRAVERTINE, A CHEMICAL LIMESTONE THAT RESEMBLES MARBLE WHEN POLISHED, COMES FROM THE EVAPORATION OF CALCIUM CARBONATE FROM FRESH OR SALT WATER. A GOOD HARD SCRUBBING CAN DESTROY THE SURFACE OF TRAVERTINE, WHICH SHOULD BE CLEANED WITH NOTHING STRONGER THAN A SPONGE AND WARM WATER.

Above: ONE WARM, NEUTRAL COLOR PREVAILS IN THIS REFINED MARBLE BATHROOM SET AMONG THE TREETOPS. THE MONOCHROMATIC COLOR SCHEME KEEPS THE FOCUS ON THE SPLENDID VIEWS AVAILABLE FROM THE WINDOWS AND THE DRAMATIC SKYLIGHT.

Above: Set into a marble-clad corner, this circular mosaic hot tub looks warm and inviting. A lace-curtained window with wooden trim, an antique wooden chest, an old-fashioned marble sculpture, and a large framed floral tapestry help to give this contemporary space a sense of antiquity.

Opposite: ALTHOUGH THESE WALLS APPEAR TO BE MADE OF DRY, UNMORTARED STONES, THE MASONS CEMENTED THE STONES TOWARD THE BACK WHERE IT WOULDN'T SHOW. THIS ANCHORING KEEPS THE STONEWORK SAFE AND MAINTAINS THE ATTRACTIVE PATTERN OF HORIZONTAL LINES IN THIS LIGHT AND AIRY TUB ROOM. AN EXTERIOR STEPPED WALL CONTINUES THE PATTERN OUTDOORS WHILE BLENDING INTO THE LANDSCAPE. THE CONSISTENT USE OF STONE AND THE BROAD EXPANSE OF GLASS SEPARATING INDOORS FROM OUT MINIMIZE THE DISTINCTION BETWEEN THE TWO AREAS.

Right: POLISHED GRANITE IS AN EXCELLENT CHOICE FOR TUB SURROUNDS AND BATHROOM FLOORS BECAUSE ITS NONPOROUS SURFACE DOES NOT STAIN WHEN WET. IT IS PARTICULARLY SUITABLE FOR SEASIDE LOCATIONS, SUCH AS THIS BEAUTIFUL HOME, BECAUSE THE SALTY AIR CANNOT DAMAGE IT.

Below: THE PALE WOOD OF THE FORMAL VANITY WITH MOSAIC TILES BRINGS A FEELING OF LIGHTNESS TO THIS AIRY BATHROOM. A MOSAIC BORDER IN RICH, EARTHY COLORS ADDS WARMTH AND INTEREST TO THE ROOM, WHILE THE GLOSSY REFLECTIVE SURFACE OF THE TRAVERTINE COUNTERTOPS AND THE LARGE MIRRORS EMPHASIZE THE OPEN QUALITY OF THE SPACE.

Above: A MONOCHROMATIC SCHEME RUNS THE RISK OF SEEMING BLAND OR FLAT, BUT SUBTLE VARIATIONS IN HUE AND TEXTURE CAN MAKE A ONE-COLOR ROOM COME TO LIFE. IN THIS SPACIOUS BATH, SOFTLY PATTERNED MARBLE IN A RANGE OF TAUPES AND BEIGES ADDS DEPTH TO THE NEUTRAL PALETTE, WHILE PLUSH CARPETING, THICK TOWELS, AND A COMFORTABLE UPHOLSTERED CHAIR PROVIDE COMFORT AND WARMTH.

Opposite: THE CLEAN LINES AND STRONG EARTHY HUES OF MUSTARD, BRICK, AND BEIGE BALANCE THE VISUAL WEIGHT OF THE BROWN STONE TUB SURROUND, FLOOR, AND COUNTER. TEAL TOWELS ADD A SPLASH OF CONTRASTING COLOR, WHILE CHROME FIXTURES MAINTAIN THE BATHROOM'S SLEEK LINES. THE COUNTER SURFACE ADJACENT TO THE MIRROR IS THE PERFECT PLACE TO DISPLAY CONTEMPORARY CRAFTS LIKE THIS STRIKING VASE FILLED WITH FLOWERS.

Durable Outdoor Details

For millennia, stone has been the material of choice for exquisite durable objects and architectural details inside and outside the home. Some early stone ornaments were made from *pietre dure*, hard semiprecious stones like agate, jasper, and lapis lazuli, cut with special gem-cutting tools. The Romans refined these ancient techniques, which experienced a second wave of popularity during the Renaissance. In the sixteenth century, Italian artists used *pietre dure* to create intricate mosaic panels for tabletops, cabinets, and other furnishings. The Florentines still make these pieces today.

Mantels, dresser tops, tables, lamp bases, and candlesticks made of marble are popular because they lend a touch of elegance to a room without requiring that the owner spend a fortune on the decor. Stone sculptures, urns, pedestals, fountains, birdbaths, and fossils can bring a sense of history to even the most modern room.

Outdoors, the creative use of stone can inject humor or mystery into a garden. With their cool, dark, damp interiors, stone grottoes recall the days of cave dwellers. Grottoes, however, often hold sophisticated surprises like mosaic floors, grotesque or humorous sculptures, a fountain or waterfall, and a place to sit and ponder the mysteries of life.

Whether formal or informal, stone patios carry the style of the house outdoors. Adorned with a jumble of flower-filled pots and comfortable chairs or benches, traditional flagstone or slate patios project warmth and cheerfulness. Colorful mosaics on a patio wall suit a Mediterranean-style villa, while a bold sculpture of either abstract or figurative design makes an effective ornament when set against the broad planes of a cubist house.

Stone can transform a common garden item into a substantial work of art. While a wooden arbor entwined

Opposite: Weathered stone has been used here to create a pool and surrounding patio with the elegance and timeless quality of an ancient Greek structure. The pale stone wall of the pool reflects the sunlight that comes through the water, creating a cool, sparkling place ideal for a morning swim before breakfast. **Above:** Marble's softness allows it to be carved in great detail. This naturalistic carving of a flowering stem from the Taj Mahal in Agra, India, is startling in its clarity and refinement.

with vines blends into its surroundings, a granite arbor has a powerfully sculptural presence both in summer, when it might be covered with climbing roses or vines, and in winter, when it may be half buried in the snow.

Fountains made of stone can affect the garden's mood tremendously. Japanese-style gardens often include fountains made of uncut stone and bamboo, which appear to have come from nature rather than the hand of man, and have a strong, elemental presence. A traditional European garden, however, might have an ornate fountain carved with cherubs, dolphins, or young maidens bearing water pitchers. Modern designs include a glistening sheet of water sliding down a polished granite wall, and a contemporary construction using the force of water to turn stone spheres in a shallow stone basin.

By looking carefully at your rooms and gardens, you'll discover new uses for stone and marble around the house. Let these materials inspire you to create something distinctive and special. Whether you live in a castle or a cottage, stone and marble can transform your home in ways both subtle and dramatic.

Above: Carved acanthus leaves encircle the base of this stone birdbath, supported by four bronze turtles on a circular stone platform. When buying stone garden ornaments, it's important to research which materials can survive the climatic extremes of your location. The same marble that lasts for millennia in Southern Italy or Greece would disintegrate in the severe climate of the American Midwest.

Above: Thousands of years ago, these marine creatures became embedded in rock. Eventually, the organic material was worn away, leaving a mold that gradually filled with limestone. These limestone casts have all the intricate details of the original creatures, but they are solid stone. Fossils such as these make wonderful decorative accents.

Opposite: A COARSE STONE WALL MAKES AN IMPOSING BACKDROP FOR THE SIMPLE BUT SOPHISTICATED FURNISHINGS ON THIS VERANDA. THE GREEN AND WHITE SOFA UPHOLSTERY LOOKS COOL IN CONTRAST WITH THE WARM STONE AND CLAY WALL, AND ITS PATTERNS OF CHECKS AND STRIPES BALANCE THE ORGANIC ELEMENTS INCLUDING THE WALL, THE WICKER FURNITURE, AND THE FLOWERS. **Above:** THIS IDYLLIC SCENE RELIES ON STONE FOR SUBSTANCE AND BEAUTY. THE COOL STONE PATIO, SET FOR AN ALFRESCO LUNCH, LOOKS PARTICU-LARLY INVITING UNDER THE SHADE OF THE GRAPE ARBOR. THE ROUGH EXTERIOR STONE WALL GIVES THE WHOLE SCENE A RUSTIC FEELING.

Left: Stone gives this terrace over the sea substance and a sense of permanence. Although the seating is lightweight and the tabletop is glass, the massive base of the table is made of carved stone and the terrace floor is a patchwork of irregularly shaped pavers. Irregular pavers are appropriate for an informal look, while straight-cut stones appear more formal.

Opposite: The design of these handsome walls reflects the shapes and colors in the surrounding landscape. Visible in the distance is a mesa, a flat-topped elevation, which looks like it was intended to be an integral part of this Southwestern landscape.

Opposite: This limestone mermaid sits in the alcove of a wall-like hedge. Stone is used in this garden not only for decorative reasons but also for purposes of line and structure. Stone steps descend to the lower level of the garden, and rough cobbles separate the path from the planting bed. **Above:** Lavish vegetation softens the hard edges of the rugged stone facade of this house. Lush plants also diminish the brightness of the white stone coping around the pool and help to blend it into its setting. The selection of coping material often determines how well a pool ultimately fits into its environment.

Opposite: THE STONE HARDSCAPE AROUND THIS DECORATIVE POOL IS INTEGRATED INTO ITS SURROUNDINGS BY MEANS OF CAREFULLY SELECTED PLANT MATERIAL. PERENNIAL GRASSES AND FLOWERS NOT ONLY THRIVE IN THE WATER BUT ALSO GROW AROUND AND THROUGH THE STONE PAVING. BEHIND THE FORE-GROUND PERENNIALS IS A DENSE PLANTING OF SHRUBS AND TREES. A STONE FROG FOUNTAIN IS A WHIMSICAL ADDITION TO THE POOL. **Right:** GARDEN FURNITURE DOESN'T HAVE TO BE EXPENSIVE TO BE BOTH USEFUL AND ATTRACTIVE. IT CAN BE AS SIMPLE AS THIS TABLE, COMPOSED OF A SLATE SLAB RESTING ON LEGS MADE FROM LIMESTONE BLOCKS AND ARCHITECTURAL FRAGMENTS.

Above: STONE IS AN INDISPENSABLE ELEMENT OF A JAPANESE-STYLE GARDEN. HERE, A STONE LANTERN AND A FOUNTAIN CONSTRUCTED FROM A STONE BASIN WITH A BAMBOO SPOUT SIT AMONG NATURAL ROCKS HARMONIOUSLY ARRANGED ON A BED OF GRAVEL. LOW CONIFERS AND AZALEAS CONTRIBUTE TO THE PEACEFUL AND REFLECTIVE MOOD OF THE GARDEN. **Opposite:** THE MOSS THAT FILLS THE CREVICES BETWEEN THESE RECTANGULAR PAVERS EASES THE TRANSITION FROM THE SOLID FURNISHINGS TO THE LUXURIANT SHRUBS AND TREES BEYOND THE PATIO. IN THIS BUCOLIC SETTING, STONE IS THE UBIQUITOUS MATERIAL FOR CONSTRUCTION. THE WIDE CURVE OF THE STONE SETTEE ECHOES THE SHAPE OF THE STONE TABLE SET INTO THE PATIO. IRISES GROW IN THE SHALLOW STONE TROUGH ON THE TABLE.

APPENDIX: PAINT AND COLOR FACTS

SELECTING THE RIGHT INTERIOR PAINT

The finish of a paint affects the look of a painted surface and impacts on its maintenance. The higher the paint's sheen, the more the texture of the painted surface will be accentuated, but the easier it will be to keep clean. Paint manufacturers use different terms to describe paint sheen, but most paints fall into one of four categories: flat, eggshell or satin, semi-gloss, and gloss.

Flat Paints

These nonreflective formulations, which tend to camouflage surface imperfections, are recommended for walls and ceilings. Since it can be challenging to remove stains from flat paints, it's wise to restrict them to low-traffic areas.

Eggshell or Satin Paints

Compared to flat paints, eggshell and satin finishes have a more lustrous appearance and are more stain-resistant. Their sheen is slight, however, making these paints attactive in rooms where a subtle shine is desired. They can be gently wiped clean.

Semi-gloss paints

Because of their higher sheen, semi-gloss paints are even easier to clean than eggshell or satin paints and are often recommended for areas vulnerable to wear and tear, including kitchens, bathrooms, hallways, and children's playrooms.

Gloss Paints

As the name implies, these paints have the highest sheen. Although the look doesn't suit all interiors and their high reflectivity emphasizes surface imperfections, these paints are among the toughest, most durable formulations. Gloss surfaces are excellent for high-traffic areas and trim such as handrails or doorjambs.

WHAT COLOR SAYS AND DOES

One of the virtues of color as a design tool is its unique ability to evoke meaningful associations, provoke particular physiological responses, or serve as a symbolic reference. These effects can all determine how color is used in a decorating scheme. Understanding the meanings of different colors is a precursor to selecting a pleasing palette. It's also just plain fun.

Red

An emphatic color, red signifies both danger and romance. It is the color of courage and conviction. Red excites: sustained exposure to red hues is believed to increase the flow of adrenaline in the bloodstream. Restaurateurs believe that red hues stimulate appetite and conversation. Red is compelling, and it can create strong architectural focal points in a room.

Yellow

The most reflective of all colors, yellow is perceived quickly—it has immediacy and urgency. Yellow cheers and lifts the spirits. It is the color most often associated with the sun; hence, it is perceived as the true color of light. Like red, yellow speeds up metabolism and is often used—in appropriate shades—for kitchens and dining rooms. The Sung Dynasty honored yellow as the imperial color, which may explain why it is symbolic of intellectual and spiritual enlightenment.

Green

Green is symbolic of life, fertility, and rebirth. Green hues seem appropriate for interiors largely because they are so abundant in nature, where they act as peacemaker, harmonizing a parade of colors. Physiologically, green is said to have a soothing effect on the eyes and mind, filtering out distractions and enhancing concentration. Greens often make good backgrounds or accents in multi-hued rooms.

Blue

Infinitely popular and multifaceted, blue looks good almost anywhere, and because it's associated with the sky and ocean, it feels natural on expansive surfaces. Blue can evoke feelings of peace and tranquility and can at other times represent sadness. Blue can be incorporated into a high-tech design scheme as easily as it can appear fresh and unpretentious. Cobalt and Wedgwood blues are particularly popular in decorating schemes. Certain Eastern cultures believe blue to be the color of immortality. The Egyptians cherished blue, and even today it remains symbolic of royalty.

Violet and Purple

Perennially popular at Easter, purple was once the color of things ecclesiastical. Roman emperors and nobles of many cultures favored purple robes as an indication of privilege and power. Some psychologists suggest that purple is the color of introspection and internalization. In design, deep shades of purple or violet are generally seen as accent colors, while lighter shades work well on larger surfaces.

Black

Always classic, black is as much of a basic element in home design as it is in the fashion world. While black is technically not a color because it is devoid of light, it does affect mood and spatial perceptions just as true colors do. Black symbolizes death and wickedness but it can also suggest elegance and opulence. Colorists, designers, and painters use black as a catalyst for achieving different shades: the process of shading, adding black to a color, makes it deeper and darker.

White

While white is the color of mourning in some cultures, in Western philosophy it is the essence of purity and fresh beginnings. White is composed of the entire spectrum of light, which accounts for its many personalities. Depending upon the shade, white can be stark and sterile or clean and refreshing, and it will generally make a small room feel significantly larger. Because white is the starting point of so many wonderful custom colors, it has been called the decorator's workhorse. The process of adding white to a hue is known as tinting.

Neutrals

These palettes are often overlooked and underrated. Neutrals are exceptionally easy to live with, and are ageless, graceful, and rarely offensive. Their subtle, unobtrusive appearance makes them an ideal foil for furnishings, art, or decorative paint treatments. Today's neutrals are often custom blended from many hues, each of which imparts its own cast and color to a painted surface as light moves across it.

Sources

PAINT

Benjamin Moore Paint Co.
51 Chestnut Road
Montvale, NJ 07645
(800) 826-2623

Dutch Boy Paints
101 Prospect Avenue
Cleveland, OH 44115
(800) 828-5669

The Glidden Co.
925 Euclid Avenue
Cleveland, OH 44115
(800) 663-8589

Pratt & Lambert Paints
P.O. Box 22
Buffalo, NY 14240
(800) 269-7728

Sherwin Williams Co.
101 Prospect Avenue
Cleveland, OH 44115
(800) 4-SHERWIN

STONE & MARBLE

Ann Sacks Tile & Stone
Portland, OR
(503) 281-7751
Website: www.annsacks.com

Country Floors
15 E. 16th Street
New York, NY 10003
(212) 627-8300

Sheldon Slate
Monson, ME
(207) 997-3615
*Slate sinks, countertops,
vanities*

Stone Forest
Department G
PO Box 2840
Sante Fe, NM 87504
(505) 986-8883
*Hand-carved granite birdbaths,
basins, fountains, lanterns,
and spheres*

Stone Legends
301 Pleasant Drive
Dallas, TX 75217
(214) 398-1199
Elegant cast stone products

Stone Magic
5400 Miller
Dallas, TX 75206
(214) 826-3606
*Cast stone mantels, from classic
to contemporary styles*

FURNISHINGS

The Bombay Company
Call for the nearest store
location.
(800) 829-7789

Broyhill Furniture Industries
Call for the nearest dealership.
(800) 3-BROYHILL

Carolina Patio Warehouse
58 Largo Drive
Stamford, CT 06907
(800) 672-8466

Charles P. Rogers Brass &
Iron Beds
55 West 17th Street
New York, NY 10011
(800) 272-7726

Crate & Barrel
Call for the nearest store
location.
(800) 323-5461

Dalton Pavilions
20 Commerce Drive
Telford, PA 18969
(215) 721-1492

Drexel Heritage Furnishings
Call for the nearest dealership.
(800) 916-1986

Ethan Allen
Call for the nearest store
location.
(800) 228-9229

French Country Living
10205 Colvin Run Road
Great Falls, VA 22066
(800) 485-1302

Kohler Co.
Call for the nearest dealership.
(800) 456-4537

Pier 1 Imports
Call for the nearest store
location.
(800) 447-4371

Plain and Fancy Custom
Cabinetry
Call for the nearest dealership.
(800) 447-9006

Spiegel
Call for the nearest dealership.
(800) 345-45000

Thomasville
401 East Main Street
Thomasville, NC 27361
(800) 650-1669

Wellborn Cabinetry, Inc.
38669 Highway 77
Ashland, AL 36251
(800) 762-4475

ACCESSORIES

The Antique Quilt Source
385 Spring View Road
Carlisle, PA 17013
(717) 245-2054

Chuctanunda Antique Co.
#1 Fourth Avenue
Amsterdam, NY 12010
(518) 843-3983

Marimekko
698 Madison Avenue
New York, NY 10021
(212) 838-3842

The Masters' Collection
40 Scitico Road
Sommersville, CT 06072
(800) 222-6827

Period Lighting Fixtures
167 River Road
Clarksburg, MA 01247
(800) 828-6990

Pottery Barn
Call for the nearest store
location.
(800) 922-5507

Sur La Table
1765 Sixth Avenue South
Seattle, WA 98134
(800) 243-0852

PHOTOGRAPHY CREDITS

©Antoine Bootz: 217, 255

©Steven Brooke: 80 (Architect: George Hernandez)

Elizabeth Whiting and Associates: 107, 153, 160, 164, 184 right, 189 left, 192 (Designer: Alexander Stoddard), 197 right, 207 left (Designer: Joan Peters), 208 left, 212, 213; ©Tommy Chandler: 221; ©Michael Dunn: 229; ©Andreas V. Einsiedel: 131, 227 (Designer: Henrietta Spencer-Churchhill), 259 (Designer: Margaret Tiffin); ©Brian Harrison: 115; ©Rodney Hyett: 111, 114, 128; ©Tom Leighton: 252, 269; ©Di Lewis: 277 (Designer: Jane Packer); ©Neil Lorimer: 110; ©Mark Luscombe-Whyte: 105; ©Spike Powell: 100 right; ©David Markson: 224 bottom, 278; ©Dennis Stone: 249; ©Tim Street-Porter: 233 (Designer: Annie Kelly), 279; ©Simon Upton: 228, 253; ©Victor Watts: 268

Esto Photographics: ©Peter Aaron: 226

Franca Speranza: 231, 262, 273; ©Nider: 230, 258, 261; ©Yvan Travert: 218; ©Alain Weintraub: 244

The Garden Picture Library: ©Janet Sorrell: 159; ©Ron Sutherland: 166, 167

©Michael Garland: 102 (Architect: Fred Fisher), 112 (Designer: Cynthia Tuverson), 123 (Designer: Lauren Elia), 126 (Designer: Kelsey Maddox), 145 (Designer: Krista Everage), 190 left (Designer: Peggy Butcher), 275 (Designer: Marylin Lightston)

©Tony Giammarino: 94

©Tria Giovan: 101, 177 right, 179, 208 right, 211 right

©Anne Gordon: 223, 229, 267

©Steve Gross/Susan Daley: 122, 124, 138 right

©Nancy Hill: 8 (Designer: Stirling Associates), 82 (Designer: Diana Sawicki), 84 (Architect: Lloyd Jafvert), 87 (Designer: The Mackintosh Group), 95 (Designer: Stirling Design Associates), 99 (Designer: Joseph Major), 100 left (Designer: Rooms of England by Pamela), 120 (Designer: Karyne Johnson/Panache Interiors), 121 (Designer: David Parker Interior Design), 145 bottom (Designer: Kitchens by Deane), 215 (Designer: Stirling Design Associates)

Houses And Interiors: ©Roger Brooks: 234; ©Simon Butcher: 247, 248; ©Steve Hawkins: 237; ©Sandra Ireland: 224 top; ©Chris Rose: 222, 225; ©Verne: 235

©image/dennis krukowski: 86 (Designer: Nancy Mannucci Inc. ASID), 96, 116 (Designer: Rolf Seckinger), 127 bottom (Designer: Tonin MacCullum Inc. ASID), 132 (Designer: Matthew Patrick Smyth Inc.), 138 left (Designer: Lisa Rose Inc.), 139 (Designer: Llemeau Et. Cie), 141 (Designer: Tonin MacCullum Inc. ASID), 174

The Interior Archive: ©Tim Beddow: 130 (Architect: Alfred Cochrane), 142 (Designer: Luecks), 153, 184 left, 201 right; ©Simon Brown: 177 left, 210 (Designer: R. Banks-Pye); ©Tim Clinch: 194 left; ©Simon McBride: 129 (Designer: Clive Jones); ©James Mortimer: 174 right (Designer: Mary Goodwyn); ©Simon Upton: 125 (Designer: Anthony Collett), 209 (Designer: Nina Cambell)

©Jessie Walker Associates: 171 (Designer: Colette McKerr), 183 bottom (Designer: Donna Aylesworth), 190 right (Designer: Mary Ellen VanBuskirk), 211 left (Designer: Janice Russillo)

©Doug Keister: 147

©David Livingston: 6 (Designer: Stone Wood), 84, 88, 91, 97, 98, 106, 109, 113, 127 top, 136, 137, 140, 143, 144, 146, 154, 175 (Designer: Sharon Campbell), 194 right, 196 (Designer: The Wiseman Group), 202 left (Designer: Nancy Scheinholtz), 235 right, 236, 238, 239 (Designer: Cathy MacFee), 240 (Designer: Stone Wood), 241, 242 left (Designer: Kitchen Artworks), 242 right (Designer: Nancy Cooper), 245 (Designer: Kathleen and Doug

INDEX